The Cat Owner's Problem Solver

How to Manage Common Behavior Problems by
Thinking Like Your Cat

Margaret H. Bonham

The Cat Owner's Problem Solver
Margaret H. Bonham

Project Team
Editor: Mary E. Grangeia
Copy Editor: Stephanie Fornino
Designer: Stephanie Krautheim
Indexer: Dianne L. Schneider

TFH Publications®
President/CEO: Glen S. Axelrod
Executive Vice President: Mark E. Johnson
Publisher: Christopher T. Reggio
Production Manager: Kathy Bontz

TFH Publications, Inc.®
One TFH Plaza
Third and Union Avenues
Neptune City, NJ 07753

Printed and bound in China
11 12 13 14 15   5 7 9 8 6 4

Library of Congress Cataloging-in-Publication Data

Bonham, Margaret H.
  The cat owner's problem solver : how to manage common behavior problems by thinking like your cat / Margaret H. Bonham.
    p. cm.
  ISBN 978-0-7938-0650-8 (alk. paper)
 1. Cats--Behavior. 2. Cats--Psychology. I. Title.
 SF446.5.B648 2008
 636.8'0887--dc22
                        2007049304

The Leader In Responsible Animal Care For Over 50 Years!®
www.tfh.com

Table of Contents

Cats are truly wondrous animals. Ever since we let them into our lives some 10,000 years ago, they have been popular household pets and adored family members. Today, cats are by far one of the most popular companion pets, only to be outranked by fish. In fact, cat ownership is at an all-time high, with more than 90 million owned in the United States alone.

Chapter 1

Understanding Cats: The Tiger Within

And yet, despite all those cat lovers out there, plenty of felines end up in shelters every year. For all the companionship and love they give us, they appear to be greatly misunderstood. Some cats may have problem behaviors caused by a lack of understanding on their owner's part. Others are homeless and ill-treated because intact individuals are left to roam, resulting in an overpopulation problem that has caused feral colonies to appear in many areas. Some people hate or fear cats, still believing superstition over fact.

So let's demystify our feline friends and see what really goes on inside their furry little heads. Then perhaps we can figure out why cats do what they do.

CAT PSYCHOLOGY 101

If we could take a look inside the feline mind, we would see a very interesting creature. But to understand cats, we must first understand how humans came to domesticate them.

Cats have been around for eons. Scientists believe that the first felines descended from a prehistoric critter called *Miacis,* who lived more than 50 million years ago. That gives them quite a head start over *Homo sapiens*, who showed up among our earliest ancestors somewhere around 4 million years ago.

Fast-forward to a bit more recently. Sometime between 5,000 and 10,000 years ago, wild cats began living with people. The most likely route toward domestication occurred when humans started banding together in agricultural villages, combining resources and growing crops such as barley and wheat. Vermin, which included rats and mice, came to fields and storehouses to eat the grain. Cats, who are opportunistic by nature, found many readily available sources of food within

these early settlements. Those cats who didn't mind humans much stuck around. Eventually, humans found that the colonies of cats that stayed near the edges of their encampments appeared to be friendly and even started to interact with them. It didn't take long before people took cats and kittens into their homes.

When comparing the cat to another domesticated species, the dog, the cat is a relative newcomer to domestication. Dogs have been domesticated for anywhere from 20,000 to 125,000 years, depending on the sources you cite. They tend to be more dependent on humans, mainly because of the many thousands of years they've been companions to us. However, one should never assume that the domestic cat will do well on her own. Although modern felines still retain a fiercely independent streak, they rely on their keepers for food and shelter. While it's true that some cats have returned to the wild (hence they are feral), most are hoping and willing to be part of our human families.

Cats in the Wild

When cats live in the wild, they tend to collect in loosely associated feral cat colonies, thus displaying the need for some kind of companionship. Not quite the solitary hunters many believe them to be, cats do crave attention and affection although on their own terms.

Yet despite their fondness for company, cats tend to be somewhat solitary in addressing their daily needs. Unlike dogs, who are descended from wolves, cats don't hunt in packs or travel after migrating game. But because they are carnivores, they must eat meat to survive. So nature endowed these sleek and stealthy felines with all the tools they need to hunt for food on their own. One look at your cat's teeth and claws, and you can see that she wasn't made for gnawing on veggies.

Nature also designed cats perfectly for their lifestyle. Their bodies, senses, and

The domestic cat is not unlike her ancient ancestor, the African wildcat, Felis silvestris lybica.

When Cats Met Humans

About half a billion house cats are believed to be in the world today, while many other species of cat and wildcat are now threatened by extinction. Why is this, you might wonder? Unlike other domesticated animals, which were tamed by people, it is thought that cats domesticated themselves, which may account for their rather notorious independent streak. These early feline ancestors survived by adapting to a new environment, which means the push for domestication came from them and not from humans. It all started about 10,000 years ago, when a few courageous wildcats crept into the first human settlements scavenging for food. Because they felt safe from predators there and were natural hunters, they found easy access to satisfying food sources in the rodents that fed on the settlers' crops. When they saw that the cats were earning their keep by ridding their fields and granaries of vermin, the settlers welcomed them and the arrival of future offspring.

instincts are primed to help them hunt and survive in the wild without help from other individuals. The domestic cat isn't very different from her wild cousins. Cats are built not for long hunts but for short, ambush-type hunts. Most of their muscles (called fast-twitch muscles) lend themselves to short, explosive bursts of energy. Cats can rotate their bodies 180 degrees, giving them a great range of motion. All these traits allow them to leap great heights, sprint and climb with ease, and chase after anything that catches their eye.

Cats are also nocturnal. They use food and sleep to recharge themselves—most adult cats sleep anywhere from 16 to 20 hours a day. Because the cat is primarily a night hunter, she is most active after sunset. Her eyes can see very well in almost total darkness. This is due to the changing shape of her pupils, which are actually more efficient than the rounded pupils we have. At night, a cat's pupils open up wider to allow her eyes to gather in more light; in the daytime, the pupils can conveniently close up to a mere slit so that she can enjoy basking in the sun without the need for sunglasses!

Why is all this important to know? It's important because you really can't separate the cat's mind from her body. When looking at your cat, you need to understand why she behaves the way she does by being aware of her primitive instincts. The cat is a hunter, and while she has had some 5,000 to 10,000 years of domestication, she is still pretty much the same creature as her ancestor, *Felis silvestris lybica,* the African wildcat. By learning your cat's natural behavior, you can think like a cat and even anticipate what may be causing her to do some of the bothersome and odd things she does. Things we think of as problem behaviors are really just natural behaviors to your cat, but with the right information at hand, you can live in harmony with your feline companion.

Why Cats Do What They Do—Understanding Common Behaviors

So now that you understand a little bit about where the domestic cat came from, we're going to look at her basic behaviors—that is, behaviors that every cat does and why she (including your feline companion) does them. Some are fairly innocuous, but others can be annoying or destructive.

Scratching is a natural behavior for cats.

Scratching

Scratching is something all cats do. It's as natural to them as breathing or eating. Cats scratch for a variety of reasons. They do it to mark their territory—that is, to let other cats know that they're around. They do it to file down their claws and keep them sharp for hunting. They do it for exercise and stretching. And they do it because they like to do it.

Because scratching is very important to them (it's how they communicate, after all), taking away that ability leaves a cat maimed and unhappy. Many problem behaviors stem from declawing cats, which is why you should never do so except under the most extreme circumstances.

Declawing isn't just the removal of the nails; it's the removal of the cat's toes up to the first knuckles. Look at your own fingers and imagine how you would feel if you were to have your fingers lopped off at the first knuckle. Not very pleasant, is it? Surgery of this sort may cause pain later.

Good Cat, Bad Cat

Contrary to what many people may think, cats do not misbehave out of spite. They simply do what's natural or what makes sense to them. To correct any problem behavior, an owner must first figure out what the cat is trying to communicate and then redirect that unwanted behavior toward an acceptable, positive behavior.

To modify your cat's behavior, you first need to catch her in the act of doing the "wrong" thing, correct her, and then show her what she should be doing instead. Try to correct the unwanted behavior as soon as you notice it, because the longer the habit continues, the harder it will be to break. In time and with enough reinforcement, your cat will learn what you expect of her, and you will be able to live in harmony with your feline friend.

Likewise, tendonectomies aren't much better. They involve cutting the tendons in the cat's paws so that she cat can't use them properly. This surgery is also a form of maiming that may cause pain later.

But the pain and maiming aren't the only reasons not to have these procedures done. A cat who has been declawed often feels afraid and vulnerable. She is mentally scarred because she has lost her ability to do things necessary for survival, and you've removed her defensive weapons. You've also removed her ability to easily cover her feces and urine when she uses the litter box. By removing her claws and part of her toes, you have unbalanced her, too—she isn't as confident about running and jumping as she once was.

Although their assertions are based on anecdotal evidence, most animal behaviorists have noted that declawing leads to more serious problems, such as marking, inappropriate urination and defecation outside the litter box, and aggression. The Cat Fanciers' Association (CFA) has written a statement regarding declawing that maintains that no cat should be declawed or subjected to tendonectomy unless the owner has a bleeding disorder or a compromised immune system (AIDS, cancer, and the like).

If you choose to have a cat, scratching comes with the territory. Later, we'll look at how to redirect scratching to more acceptable targets to keep your house looking good.

Marking

Marking, that is, spraying a vertical object with urine, is a common behavior in cats. While we find this highly inappropriate, cats do it as a way to communicate with each other. Both male and female cats spray/mark, but intact male cats do it far more often than neutered female cats. A cat who sprays is advertising her presence and telling the world that this is her territory.

Naturally, owners consider marking an unwanted

behavior, but it usually occurs when a cat feels insecure or threatened by other cats or new objects. New people, new pets, and new furniture can all cause a cat to spray, as can the presence of unfamiliar cats outside your home.

Marking should never be confused with inappropriate urination, which occurs strictly on the floor.

Meowing

The word "meow" is synonymous with cats because this is the vocalization we've all come to recognize as being feline. However, you may be surprised to learn that most wild and feral cats don't meow that much. Meowing, it seems, is a domestic cat's way of getting our attention.

Some cats are naturally mouthy. Oriental breeds, such as Siamese, are very chatty. When dealing with people, cats do what we react to most—they make verbal sounds. Our reaction to their vocalizations causes them to meow even more. So when your cat is meowing loudly at her food bowl, she's calling you to come feed her. Makes sense, doesn't it?

Purring

We've all heard that contented rumble in our cat's throat. A vibrating, low thrum that says she is happy and content. But cats purr for a variety of reasons: when they're happy, when they're sick and injured, when they're giving birth, when they're nervous or afraid, and even when they're dying. So although we may know that cats purr, we don't really understand why.

Many behaviorists think that cats purr because it is a comforting sound. For example, a fearful or sick cat may purr to console and calm herself when things are scary or painful—she's sort of telling herself that everything will be all right. A purr can also be a way of saying "I need a friend to help me feel good." At the same time, when your cat is happy and contented, she may be saying "I'm really glad to have a friend like you, and you make me happy." Confusing, isn't it?

If that weren't enough, to this day, scientists don't completely understand the mechanism behind the purr. They know it has something to do with breathing and the cat's voice box, but exactly how it works remains a mystery. But there's no mystery when your cat is sitting in your lap purring sweetly!

Rubbing Up Against You or Objects

If you share your life with a cat, I'm sure you've experienced this quite a bit: Your feline friend comes over to you and rubs her head and face against you or maybe rubs her body up against your legs. What's up with that?

You probably won't be surprised to learn that it's a sign of affection. Cats don't only rub up against people because they like them but also to claim them. You see, cats have special sebaceous glands in their cheeks, mouth, and chin that secrete a unique hormone that marks you with their own particular scent. (We can't smell it, but cats can). When your cat rubs against you, she is identifying you as her special human and laying claim on you, just in case any unfamiliar cats may be present.

Likewise, cats will rub up against objects around the house to harmlessly mark them as part of their territory. It reminds them where their boundaries are and also lets any stray animals know what's going on.

Kneading

You're spending some quality time with your kitty. She's lying down in your lap and purring mightily, when suddenly she starts moving her paws back and forth in a rhythmic motion, like she's kneading bread. Her sharp claws may go into your leg and come out in a quick motion—not enough to scratch but enough to feel as though you have needles pricking you.

As you may have guessed, kneading is one of the greatest compliments your cat can pay you. She is telling you that she trusts you and that she feels happy and secure around you. She used to do this when she was with her mom—and when she does this, she's telling you that you're just like a mom to her. Pretty cool, huh?

Chasing Moving Objects

One of the fun things about living with cats is that they are curious and playful.

If you wiggle a feather or a toy, your cat is bound to follow it. It all starts innocuously enough. You wiggle a teaser toy or feather, and suddenly your cat's head snaps around and begins following it. Her tail whips from side to side, and she crouches down, ready to pounce. So why does she do that?

Cats are hardwired to hunt. They recognize certain movements as being similar to those of their natural prey, whether it's mice, rats, or birds. Your cat knows that these toys aren't really prey, but they still excite her hunting instincts, so she goes after them to keep herself entertained and active.

You can teach your cat to go after the right kinds of "prey" by encouraging her to play with teaser toys (feathers and other objects on a stick), fishing toys (objects on a fishing pole), and other toys that keep your hands and feet out of reach.

Bringing in Dead Animals

If your cat has ever blessed you with dead rodents or pieces of them on your doorstep or somewhere in the house, you may say "Ugh." After all, it's pretty disgusting to have such a gift left for you. But let's look at it from a cat's perspective.

Playing with toys stimulates your cat's highly developed prey drive.

Cats are hunters, and they are true carnivores, meaning that they can't live without consuming meat. This is because they need an amino acid called taurine, which is only available to them in meat. Their bodies don't manufacture it, so they must get it from an outside source, and plant matter does not provide this nutrient.

Cats hunt because it is in their nature to do so. When your cat brings you a mouse or part of one, she's sharing the hunt with you. Indeed, she may be training you to hunt because you appear incapable of doing so yourself. When cats don't have animals to hunt, they'll sometimes leave bits of food from their plate or even a toy mouse for you. When your feline housemate does this, thank her profusely. After all, she's deemed you worthy to share in her meal.

Catnip Kick

Catnip (*Nepeta cataria*), an herb that comes from the mint family, has been around since the Middle Ages. It was used to treat colds, flu, nervousness, bladder problems, diarrhea, and other maladies. While people don't get the same "kick" from catnip that cats do, it does have a relaxing and sedating effect when consumed in tea. Cats enjoy this temporary mood-enhancing, natural, and harmless substance and will have a ball rolling around the house in fits of delight.

Reacting to Catnip

You go to the local pet-supply store and pick up some toys for your cat. A few of them are scented with catnip. After bringing them home, your cat goes wild over one of the toys, tossing it up and down and playing wildly with it. Maybe she rubs the catnip toy against her face. You may be wondering why she does that.

Catnip, or *Nepeta cataria*, is a type of plant that produces a substance known as nepetalactone, which is found in the leaves, stems, and seeds. It produces a mild high but is completely harmless to cats. When eaten, it has a sedative-like effect. (If you have some catnip tea, it will calm you down.) Felines seem to be particularly sensitive to it; dogs and humans don't react to it in the same way.

Only some cats are reactive to catnip—perhaps it's a hereditary predisposition. Young kittens do not react to it either—it appears that it only affects more mature individuals. Some owners, however, have reported that cats who showed no reaction to catnip initially can suddenly grow to like it.

Burying Waste

Cats, as you might already know, learn to use the litter box with ease, and they are very tidy about it. Most domestic cats bury their waste because it's highly instinctual. They do this to conceal their presence from more aggressive and dominant felines and from predators.

In the wild, this was probably a pretty good trait to have. After all, advertising you're around to the bully on the block doesn't get you brownie points—it gets you beaten up. So covering one's tracks and being secretive was probably a smart evolutionary move on the cat's part to ensure her survival. After all, if a predator can't find you, it can't catch you.

CATS AT HOME

Found in all corners of the world, domestic cats have been living with us for thousands of years, and yet they've managed to retain their independence, natural instincts, and an aura of mystery. And despite their occasional pesky behaviors, cats are wonderful companions as far as pets go. They are intelligent creatures that adapt quickly to almost any lifestyle, and they are content to live wherever you do. They are self-reliant and can be left alone for hours at a time, but they will rush to greet you when you come home. But as any cat lover knows, they are unique individuals, with each one having distinct personality traits and behaviors. Once you understand cat behavior, however, you will be able to deal with any problem behaviors you are faced with—you'll feel like you have the secret to successful cat training. More importantly, though, you'll make life happier and healthier for your feline friend and for yourself.

SO NOW YOU KNOW…

- Cats have ancient origins going back millions of years.
- Cats were domesticated fairly recently compared to dogs—only 5,000 to 10,000 years ago.
- Cats are likely descended from the African wildcat, *Felis silvestris lybica*.
- A cat's claws were designed by nature for a reason. She needs them to function normally, so you should never declaw a cat because it is both painful and cruel.
- Cats do not misbehave out of spite. They simply do what comes naturally to them.
- Understanding feline behavior and psychology can help you understand your domestic cat's nuances.
- Most unwanted behaviors can be replaced with acceptable ones with patience and positive training.

You have happily shared your home with your kitty for awhile now, but for some reason she has started behaving badly. She may be scratching the furniture or eliminating outside the litter box. Or maybe she's attacking you whenever you walk into the room, which is a really unsettling problem.

Chapter 2

Bad Kitty!: What to Do When Your Cat Has a Problem

But before you start thinking that your beloved feline hates you or that she is maladjusted, be aware that she is probably behaving in this way for a legitimate reason. That unwanted behavior isn't motivated by spite or jealousy, and your cat isn't punishing you for something you've done or not done. On the contrary, chances are she is acting out due to certain health or environmental issues.

IS YOUR CAT REALLY BAD?

The first problem we humans have is that we tend to anthropomorphize our animals. We think that because people would behave in this or that fashion that our pets must behave in a likewise manner, or that they know right from wrong. If I had a nickel for every time someone said to me "She knows what she's supposed to do, but she just doesn't care…" or "Look at her, she's hiding because she feels guilty," I'd be very rich indeed!

Cats don't react emotionally in the way humans do. While they do feel fear, pain, hate, and love, they don't process information in the same way. In other words, they are not likely to do things on the basis of "right" or "wrong," even if they understand that their behaviors will produce some sort of cause and effect. However, if the relationship between the action and its particular effect doesn't add up, they're unlikely to link the two.

So let's say that you've just noticed that your cat has urinated on the wall. You grab her, march her over to the spot, show it to her, and then swat her rump. Do you think that she understands what this means or that it will do any good? If you've tried it—and I highly recommend that you *don't* do this—you'll know that it has little effect on your cat's behavior, save perhaps causing her to run and hide under the bed whenever she sees you. This is because your action (swatting her) is presented in no clear context to her. She doesn't connect the dots between urinating on the wall and being punished for a behavior that is otherwise natural to her. Rather, she decides that you're a very nasty person and that you should be avoided. Lovely.

In reality, your cat may be spraying the wall due to insecurity issues. Perhaps you brought home a new cat or a new piece of furniture. Cats hate change so much that they can get a little wonky when something outside of their normal circumstances occurs. If some aspect of your cat's environment has changed, she will want to assert herself and will do so by marking her territory. She's not even thinking about you or the fact that she's ruined the drapes or the paint on the wall. What's more, the scent of her spray is a source of familiarity and comfort to her, and if you don't get rid of the smell, she'll do it again because that object or space belongs to her now—it's her territory.

A cat's age can also impact her behavior. For instance, adolescent cats go through an awkward stage of insecurity and experimentation, and they don't "grow up and settle down" until they are a year old. They may mark or spray to test their boundaries. Likewise, senior cats may often develop problem behaviors, such as house soiling, due to physical and emotional changes you may not be aware of right away. More often than not, your cat's behavior has nothing to do with being spiteful or angry.

Cats don't see the world as we do, but you (being a human with that big brain of yours) can figure out what's going on in your pet's mind with a little patience and knowledge. It's not really a mystery. You just need to understand your cat's map of reality and see how her instinctual behavior may be at the root of those

Understanding why your cat is misbehaving and then getting to the root of the problem is the best way to correct unwanted behavior.

inappropriate behaviors. In most cases, she has either been doing something natural to her that needs retraining, or she is just reacting to change.

EXAMINING THE PROBLEM

Cats are fairly simple creatures once you get right down to it. As suggested, in most cases one of two things occurred to cause your cat's inappropriate behavior:

- The behavior is one that she has always engaged in but has not been discouraged from performing.

or

- The behavior is caused by some internal (medical condition) or external (environmental) situation.

Hypothetically, correcting the problem is easy: Either change the behavior by redirecting it toward a behavior you want, or figure out what has changed in your cat's environment so that you can adjust it and eliminate the problem. That's it. But naturally, this is sometimes easier said than done.

Regardless of the degree of the problem, you have to be fair to your feline friend and consider all the possible root causes of the unwanted behavior in question. However, before you start trying to diagnose what is going on, your first approach should be a trip to the veterinarian. While some vets may not have experience dealing with behavioral problems, they do have knowledge about diseases and conditions that can mimic them. Consulting a vet helps you rule out whether a biological issue is contributing to the situation, which certainly simplifies the task at hand somewhat.

DID YOU KNOW?

Many litter box issues tend to be biological rather than behavioral in nature. Cats can be suffering from a medical problem such as a urinary tract infection, which can lead to urination outside the box. By having your veterinarian evaluate your cat, you can rule out any medical issues and perhaps solve the problem before having to resort to calling in a behaviorist.

Visiting the Vet

As mentioned earlier, behavioral problems are often symptoms of biological problems. For example, a cat who doesn't use her litter box all the time may be trying to tell you it hurts to use it for one reason or another. Cats don't understand why they are not feeling well, so they tend to look for something in their environment that is a source of the discomfort they are feeling. Because cats externalize a lot of the blame, one who is in pain when she uses the litter box may think that there's something wrong with it. Or if she hurts when you pet her, she may think that you are hurting her, which may cause her to lash out at you.

This may not be completely logical to you, but to a cat it makes complete sense. Therefore, it's wise to have her checked out by a vet to determine if she has any health issues.

What Your Vet Needs to Know

When you make an appointment with your vet, the first thing you should do is provide him with a good description of what your cat has been doing. Be sure to include as much information as you can. While the description "She doesn't use her litter box" is a start, it doesn't really give him much to go on. In this instance, try to watch your cat as she uses the litter box. Is she straining? Does she look uncomfortable? When does she urinate outside the box? Is she spraying on a vertical surface or on the floor? How does she act when you see her? Is she hiding all the time? Is she playful or lethargic? All these things will help your vet determine what to look for.

If your vet examines your cat and can't find anything wrong (or doesn't find anything specific), don't rule out a biological cause just yet. Some conditions might not be caught in the first visit. At this early stage, you're going to have to do some homework to figure out what is ailing your cat.

One word of caution: Although it doesn't happen often, in more serious

A sudden bout of unwanted behavior could be an indication of a medical or emotional problem, so have your cat examined by a vet.

Curious but Cautious

Cats may be curious, but they are cautious to a fault and they hate change. Being sensitive creatures, they can develop seemingly irrational fears about all sorts of things. Some fear is natural and self-protecting; some is irrational and eventually gets out of hand. Some cats are just shy.

Just as the source of these fears or anxieties can be diverse, so can the way in which problem behaviors manifest themselves. For example, some cats may run away, hide under the bed or in a closet, freeze, hiss, or even attack you. Others may urinate outside of their litter box.

The first step in dealing with problem behavior is to identify any emotional or environmental factors that may be causing stress. The most common are separation anxiety, a new person or pet in the home, a change of environment, boredom, being weaned too early, and loud noises. If the stressor can be removed, do so promptly. If not, you may be able to get your cat used to the presence of the stressor by gradually exposing her to it at a time when she is feeling relaxed; then, gradually increase the exposure until she is comfortable with it. It is also beneficial to enrich her environment as much as you can by providing her with toys, climbing apparatus, and exercise. Medication should be a last resort to solving a problem behavior.

cases a vet may suggest a solution that you feel is not at all appropriate for your cat. For example, he might recommend administering a drug like Prozac to limit the behavior, but you would prefer a less drastic alternative. Most feline experts consider Prozac and other medications a last resort, preferring to try to fix the problem rather than throw medications at it. If you're looking for other options, consult a cat behaviorist first to see if perhaps the problem can be remedied through behavior modification.

DETERMINING THE CAUSE OF THE PROBLEM

Determining the cause of any unwanted behavior often requires a bit of sleuthing. If it's something your cat has always done, such as scratching or hopping up on the countertop, it's simply a matter of retraining her—after all, you may never have trained her not to do those things to begin with! Or maybe it's something as simple as changing the type of litter box or litter your cat is using (or not using).

But usually, bad behavior occurs because something uncomfortable triggers it. Cats dislike change, so their behavior will center on trying to cope with the problem and figuring out how to make it go away. Take notes on what you think may have caused the behavior, and watch closely what your cat does and where and when she does it. You'll need to look at all these factors to determine how to solve the problem.

Regardless of what your cat does wrong, never yell at her or hit her. Besides being cruel, this will not correct the mistake and in most cases will make her distrust you, which could lead to even more problems. To modify your cat's behavior, you need to catch her in the act and then teach her what she should be doing instead. You should also correct unwanted behavior as soon as you notice it because it can be difficult to break a bad habit the longer it continues. By using positive training and reinforcement, your cat will soon learn what's expected of her.

Once you determine the source of problem behavior, you can teach your cat all sorts of useful commands using clicker training, which will also help you bond with your cat.

Should you need expert intervention, a pet behaviorist is someone who understands animals well and can help you properly retrain your cat.

Tools for Clicker Training

The basic tools for clicker training are pretty simple. You need a clicker (available at many pet-supply stores or on the Internet), a target stick (an unsharpened pencil or a pen with its cap on works just fine), and a handful of yummy treats or something your cat really loves to play with.

Now, before you object and say that your cat is truly finicky, think about the things she is willing to mug you for. Tiny bits of tuna or cooked beef (bite-sized pieces) or a taste of her favorite cat treat can be good motivators. Or if she's more the playful type, a quick bat at her favorite tickler toy works well.

The point is to find something for which your cat is willing to work. It may take a bit of trying, but once you figure out at least two motivators, switch between them occasionally to prevent boredom.

A note of caution about the clicker: Some cats find the noise a bit scary. So if you have a fraidy cat, cover the clicker with your palm to soften the noise before clicking it.

Getting Started With the Clicker

By now you have a clicker, some yummy treats, and a target stick. Put the target stick away for the moment because we're going to focus just on teaching your cat the clicker for now.

- Find a time when your cat is a bit hungry, maybe before her meal. Click the clicker once and give her a treat.
- Click and treat. Click and treat. Remember, you'll be handing out a lot of treats, so keep them very *tiny*.
- Watch your cat as you click and treat. At some point, she should be showing interest and looking up expectantly whenever she hears the click. That's when you know she's associated the clicker with the food reward. This is what you want.
- Quit after five minutes, whether your cat has figured it out or not.

Sometimes it takes a cat longer than one session to figure out how the clicker works. Don't despair. Try again in a few hours and see if she'll figure it out then. If she doesn't seem to get it yet, plan to train the next day. Remember to keep training sessions short so that your cat doesn't get bored or frustrated, and always end every session on a high note with praise and a reward.

Varying Clicker Timing

Once your cat figures out the clicker, you can move on to the next step: varying the timing between the click and the treat.

- Click the clicker once and wait for three seconds. Your cat should be looking at you expectantly.
- Give your cat the treat.
- Now click again and vary the wait time. Give your cat the treat after she has waited a bit longer.
- Continue to vary the lengths of time between the click and the treat so that your cat learns that she'll get the reward regardless of how long the click takes to occur. That way, if you can't treat right away, she'll know that she will eventually be rewarded for being patient.
- Practice this several times until you know your cat has figured it out. It may take several five-minute sessions before she feels confident about food coming with every click.
- If your cat forgets how the clicker works or she acts bored at any time, return to the first lesson to be sure that she has a firm grasp of it.

Although you can't change your cat's natural, instinctive behaviors, you can teach her how to adapt those behaviors so that both of you can live happily together.

Varying How You Offer the Treat

Next, teach your cat that the treat doesn't always come directly from your hand. This may not be a big deal, but if you toss a bit of a treat to your cat, you want her to recognize that this is still part of the click-and-treat training exercise. This will also enable you to expand on her training later by introducing different tasks that she will learn to associate with the clicker.

- Choose a treat your cat likes that isn't too wet or sticky.
- Click and place the treat directly in front of her. She may need encouragement to pick up the treat.
- Once she takes that treat, click and place another treat slightly to her right. If she's confused about where the treat is, show it to her with your hand and then place it in its spot. Remember to encourage her to take the treat.
- Click and place another treat slightly to her left. Again, if there's any confusion about where it is, show it to her. This isn't a game of hide-and-seek.
- Continue clicking and treating, placing treats in various locations until your cat gets the idea that treats can appear anywhere, not just from your hand.
- If your cat isn't easily startled by things, you may want to try tossing the treat toward her. Just don't hit her or have the treat get so close that it scares her. Otherwise, you'll set back your training and will have to start the clicker training process all over again.

The best way to train a cat is through positive reinforcement. Many trainers and behaviorists use clickers and cat treats to correct unwanted behavior.

Remember to practice this in five-minute lessons (no more than two five-minute lessons a day), and refrain from going longer; this will keep her interested and willing to participate again in the future. End every session on a high note with praise and a reward.

Teaching the Target Stick

Now that your cat has learned the basics of clicker training, it's time to add the target stick. The target stick is used to help move your cat and focus her attention on where you want her to be. The target stick is also called a touch stick, so the words can be used interchangeably.

TOO SMART FOR THEIR OWN GOOD

Cats are clearly different than dogs, and sometimes it's hard to figure them out. That's probably because cats walk a fine line between being bored and being overstimulated. Cats are highly evolved creatures who learned to be self-sufficient to survive. As a result, they have superior senses, they learn quickly, and they have great problem-solving skills. And although they may ignore things that don't interest them, at times their environment is just too exciting for them—especially in our modern world.

Cats prefer stability. They need consistency in all things: mealtimes, your comings and goings, and attention to their litter box. But they are also highly intelligent, intensely curious animals who need appropriate stimulation. Outdoor cats get plenty of this on their own, but indoor cats will need you to supply them with a reason for being happy and sane. By providing the following, you can help prevent problem behaviors before they start:

- **Exercise:** You can help keep your cat from becoming bored or distressed by giving her plenty of exercise. Outdoor cats are less likely to display neurotic behavior, but even indoor cats can be kept sufficiently busy to be content and well adjusted.

- **Attention:** Not only should you keep your cat company, but it's also important to "listen" to your cat. Her signs of distress may be subtle, but if you catch trouble brewing before it erupts, you'll both be better off.

- **Toys and adventures:** Cats are intelligent creatures who like interesting things to do. Help them by giving them plenty of interactive toys and an opportunity to explore the world "outside the box," even if it's limited to a window through which they can observe what's going on outside their territory.

- **Healthful diet:** Nutritional deficiencies or oversupplementation can ruin even the best cat's disposition, so a healthy, appropriate feline diet is essential.

- **Health care:** Certain diseases can make cats act out. Make sure that your cat has frequent checkups to maintain good health.

Clickers

A clicker is a small plastic or metal device held in the hand that makes a clicking sound when pressed. Used in clicker training animals, the sound is a marker signal that tells the pet the precise moment she has done something right. Paired with a reward, this training method works well, especially with a self-interested animal such as a cat, because it gives the pet something she actively wants to work for (usually a tasty treat) while reinforcing appropriate behaviors in the process. By relying on continuous positive reinforcement rather than punishment, this clear form of communication is a humane and highly effective way to correct undesirable behavior. In fact, with the aid of a clicker, some treats, and a little bit of patience, you can teach an animal any behavior that she is physically and mentally capable of doing—even tricks. Try it and see!

- Start by showing the target stick (you can use the blunt end of a pencil or pen) to your cat. If she appears disinterested, it's perfectly okay to wiggle it around on the floor like a toy. (Just be careful of your fingers because she may pounce, or get a longer stick if you want to prevent this.)
- When your cat grabs for the stick or touches it with her nose, click and treat. She may seem surprised by this, so if she's not sure what's happening, try showing her the target stick again and click and treat when she touches it.
- Vary clicking and treating for both paw and nose.
- You can then add a marker word, such as "paw" when she touches it with her paw or "nose" when she touches it with her nose.
- When your kitty is confident with the target stick, you can move onto training other behaviors such as "sit" or "go to a special place."

Training the Sit

Teach a cat to sit? You might be thinking that I'm kidding, but I'm not. You can do this either with a target stick or a bit of a treat.
- Have your target stick ready—or a treat, if you're luring your cat.

- Get your cat's attention by having her nose the target stick, then click and treat. If using a treat, get her attention by showing her the treat.
- Bring the target stick or the treat up and over her head, holding it just above her nose so that she follows it backward until she sits down. Click and treat.
- You may have to try a few times to get her to sit, but once you do, click and treat.
- After your cat starts sitting, you can add a marker command, such as "Sit."

Once she responds to the verbal command repeatedly, you can begin to phase out the target stick (or lure treat) and rely solely on the command.

Teaching "Go to a Special Place"

This command is very useful for owners who wish to have their cat go to a particular place without fuss, such as her bed, a cat tree, or even a cat carrier. You can use either a treat or the target stick to get your cat to do this.

- Show your cat the target stick or food. When she touches it, click and treat.
- Move the target stick a little bit away from her (or use the food lure). When your cat touches it or follows it, click and treat again.
- Keep moving the target stick or lure a little each time, clicking and treating until you get your cat moving toward the place you want her to go.
- When your cat arrives at the desired location, click and give her a "jackpot treat"—that is, give her many rewards (a few treats, a treat and a toy, etc.) for getting there.
- You will have to practice this several times.
- In the next few sessions, add the marker word for the place you wish your cat to go, such as "tree" or "bed."
- In the final stages of training, reduce the number of intermediate steps between the place your cat starts out and where you want her to go. Eventually, she will simply respond to the command alone.

Using the Clicker to Get What You Want

Clicker training is great for cats because it challenges them while simultaneously giving them new behaviors to replace the old, unwanted behaviors—a plus for any kitty and her owner! When thinking up new things to do with the clicker, break down what you want your cat to do into its most basic components. It's relatively easy to get a cat to follow a target stick, but it's harder to get her to do more complex tasks, such as jumping through a hoop. Training more difficult tasks in this way will help you achieve more success with your cat than you might ever have imagined. Have fun!

GETTING PROFESSIONAL HELP

If you feel that a problem behavior has gotten of control and you have not had any success with the methods you've tried using to correct it, it may help to seek out professional services.

Consulting a Behaviorist

While it may sound funny to talk to a professional counselor about a badly behaving cat, consider it. After all, people are willing to consult a dog trainer for a misbehaving dog.

Should you need expert intervention, a pet behaviorist is someone who understands animals well and can tell you how to properly retrain your cat. Quite often, he can assess particular situations and suggest remedies that you can implement yourself at home. In most cases, a good behaviorist is also willing to work with you and your veterinarian to first make sure that the root cause isn't biological. He'll then make recommendations on how to best resolve your cat's problem.

How to Find a Pet Behaviorist

Finding a pet behaviorist can be a little daunting. After all, the local directory won't necessarily have a listing called "Cat Behaviorist," so where do you start?

One place to try is the International Association of Animal Behavior Consultants (IAABC) at www.iaabc.org. This organization includes certified professionals who consult for a fee. If there isn't a behaviorist in your area, you might want to contact the one closest to where you live to see if he'd be willing to do a phone consultation or if he can recommend another behaviorist within a reasonable distance from your home.

Another resource is your veterinarian. Although not all vets are behaviorists, yours may be able to give you a referral or direct you to an organization that could inform you of a reputable practice in your area.

If you're stumped, try contacting an animal clinic in your area that specializes in cats, and ask if it can recommend anyone. Other places to try include shelters, cat rescues, breed societies, and cat-owning friends. If that yields nothing, you may have to do an Internet search in your state using the words "cat behavior."

Regardless of how you get into contact with a behaviorist, be aware that there are no licensing requirements in any state—anyone can hang out a shingle, which is a pretty scary thought. So before you hire someone, ask these questions:

- Are you a member of the IAABC or another animal behaviorist organization? (Being a member is not necessary, but it may show the person's professional level.)
- How many clients do you see yearly, on average?
- How many years have you been in practice as a behaviorist?
- Do you have any degrees or certifications? (PhD, DVM, VMD, or certifications important in this field.)
- Have you published any literature on cat behavior (articles or books)?
- Can you provide references from colleagues?
- Can you provide references from clients?
- Do you work with particular veterinarians or veterinary colleges?

If the behaviorist acts insulted or angry over your questions, look elsewhere. Good behaviorists will be happy to provide credentials because they want to help you and your pet. They're also aware that you are concerned about the welfare of your animal and that you are looking for someone who will help solve the problem and not compound it.

SO NOW YOU KNOW...

- Bad behavior may have biological roots.
- The first step to determining the cause of your cat's problem is a trip to the veterinarian.
- If the vet doesn't find anything wrong, there may still be a biological issue that is not yet apparent.
- In difficult cases, a certified behaviorist can more readily identify the source of unwanted behaviors and successfully retrain your cat.

Now that you have assessed the likely source of your cat's problem behavior, it's time to begin the work of creating the space and conditions that will help her become a better-behaved companion. How a cat acts depends a great deal on the overall environment in which she lives daily.

Chapter 3

Kitty Feng Shui: Creating the Right Environment for Your Cat

Believe it or not, there's a type of kitty feng shui that you can practice in your home to ensure that your feline companion is comfortable, secure, and living in harmony with her natural instincts as well as her human family. The decision to allow your cat to spend time outdoors will also impact how well she adapts to domestic life. So let's begin by first examining the pros and cons of having an indoor/outdoor cat.

INSIDE OR OUT?

A huge debate rages over whether cats should live only indoors or indoors and outdoors. Proponents of the indoor-only crowd cite the following benefits:

- Your cat is unlikely to get lost wandering away from home.
- Your cat won't be exposed to outdoor dangers, including cars, aggressive dogs, and people who dislike cats.
- Your cat won't be killed by roaming predators, such as coyotes, foxes, or hawks.
- Your cat won't be exposed to diseases from other cats, including feline leukemia (FeLV), feline immunodeficiency virus (FIV), and feline infectious peritonitis (FIP).
- Your cat will be in less danger from parasites, including heartworm, which will kill a cat if contracted. Your cat is also less likely to have fleas and ticks, which can make you sick if you contract diseases from these parasites as well.
- Your cat won't get sick from eating trash. She won't get sick or die from drinking out of a pool with antifreeze in it. She also won't accidentally eat poisons that are left out for mice, and she won't eat mice that have eaten these poisons.
- Your cat won't get into fights with other cats. She also won't mate with other cats, if intact.
- Your cat is less likely to kill animals such as birds and rodents, and she won't bring them back to you as a present.

DID YOU KNOW?

According to the Humane Society of the United States (HSUS), cats who roam outdoors often don't live past five years of age. An indoor cat, on the other hand, can live to 20 or more.

The reasons for keeping a cat indoors are indeed many. However, let's look at the reasoning behind letting a cat roam. Personally, I find that the dangers far outweigh the benefits, but we'll look at both sides:

- Cats like to explore different places. Without time outside, cats can get bored.
- Cats can get fat living indoors. They spend much of their time asleep because there's not a lot to do.
- Your cat will often do her business outside, thus eliminating the need for a litter box.
- Your cat will catch mice and eliminate the rodent population in your area.

But I Want an Outside Kitty...

Even though you may think that you're doing your kitty a favor, letting her roam freely and away from home can be deadly. According to the Humane Society of the United States (HSUS), outdoor cats seldom live past the age of five due to the hazards they face when unsupervised outdoors. Indoor cats, on the other hand, can live up to 20 years with good care.

The major advantage of keeping your cat indoors is safety. If your pet is roaming outdoors unsupervised, you have no control over what or whom she encounters.

Another factor to consider is that many of your neighbors may think outdoor cats are a nuisance. A cat will often decide that the neighbor's garden is a better place to use as a litter box than the one in her own home. If your neighbor sees your cat watching the birds by her feeder, she may do something about it. And believe it or not, there are still a lot of people in the world who simply dislike cats in general.

If you insist on having an outdoor kitty, none of my arguments are likely to dissuade you. However, I'm hoping that you consider using a fence or a containment system that will at least make your cat's environment safer. It won't totally eliminate the dangers, but taking these steps can help reduce them substantially. What's more, your neighbors won't be upset with you.

Kitty Fences and Enclosures

Letting your pet cat roam outdoors is just plain risky. However, if you have the right kind of fencing or enclosure, she may be able to occasionally enjoy the great outdoors. Bear in mind that normal fencing won't dissuade a cat from jumping or climbing, and it won't dissuade a predator from attacking your pet. She is also susceptible to parasites and other natural dangers. But if you want to provide some sun and fresh air, she needs to be in a safe environment.

Cat fences work primarily through a sort of optical illusion: Even though they are sturdy, they look dangerous and thus dissuade your cat from climbing them.

Cat Fencing

Cats don't like anything that doesn't look sturdy. This is due to their inherent distrust of objects that look like they're too flimsy to support them. Cat fencing is intentionally made to look and feel precarious. When cats put their paws on it, it moves in awkward ways, making it impossible for them to climb it. Because most felines will be discouraged from climbing it, they can be kept safe within the confines of your backyard.

As a responsible pet owner, make sure that your cat is never allowed outdoors without constant supervision. Monitor her closely so that she doesn't get into any trouble, and don't let her wander off. Safer options may include providing a safe outdoor enclosure or taking your cat out on a leash.

There are many types available; you can find most of them on the Internet. Some are freestanding, while others require you to have a fence already available to which you attach it.

There are also prefabricated, portable enclosures available so that your cat can enjoy the outdoors on a deck or balcony in relative safety. You can check them out at the following websites:

- Affordable Cat Fence—www.catfence.com
- Cat Enclosure Kit—www.cdpets.com
- Cat Fence-In—www.catfencein.com
- Kittywalk—www.kittywalk.com
- Purr…fect Cat Fence—www.purrfectfence.com

Unless you have a Houdini cat, putting up a fence or placing her in an enclosure ensures that she won't get lost, bother the neighbors, or stroll out into the street to get run over by passing cars. Although these containment systems aren't predator-proof, which means an unsupervised cat can still be injured or killed if an animal gets into them, she is far safer and more secure than when roaming freely. What's more, your kitty will get a taste of the great outdoors in a relatively controlled environment.

Barn Cats

Many people living in rural areas have barn cats—cats who are kept mainly for rodent control. Most of them are feral or nearly feral, meaning that they really aren't bonded to their owners and will seldom bond well with people. Be aware that if you have a cat colony such as this, your cats are unlikely to live much past eight years of age due to diseases, parasites, and predators.

If you keep barn cats, consider spaying and neutering them to limit the overpopulation problem. Many people employ trap/neuter/release programs to reduce the numbers of feral cats living in their communities. These folks can advise you how to live-trap the animals without harming them. Also, plan to vaccinate all outdoor cats to prevent the spread of dangerous diseases such as rabies.

Becoming an Indoor Cat

Living as an indoor pet can be challenging for any feline, especially if she was once used to being an outdoor explorer. Even if your feline has always lived inside, you may be wondering if she wouldn't just be better off as an indoor/outdoor cat.

First of all, what about that nagging problem of boredom? While cats do sleep somewhere between 16 and 20 hours a day, there are at least 4 to 8 hours in which your cat needs something with which to keep herself entertained and exercised. After all, there's not much to do in a big, lonely house except get into trouble scratching, climbing on counters, and rummaging through your things. But you can shoo away your kitty's boredom and frustration with all sorts of healthy and engaging activities. Cat scratchers, cat trees, toys, and cat houses are all great fun for your cat. Playing with your cat daily and giving her something to do while you're away from home will chase the outdoor blues away fast enough. Does she have a favorite place to sit? Try putting a perch on a windowsill where she can lie down and enjoy the view. And don't forget, the best entertainment is always another cat!

CREATING THE RIGHT INDOOR ENVIRONMENT

Whatever the reason, you've decided that you want to keep your cat indoors. Good for you! The good news is that cats are basically homebodies. They like to hang out in the comfort of their own territory. But just because they like being at home doesn't mean that they don't like and need variety. On the contrary! Cats love new things to investigate, chase, pounce, scratch, and whatnot. So let's look at how to set up a cat-friendly home. It's probably easier than you think.

Cat Toys (or How to Drive Yourself Crazy Without Even Trying)

Providing your cat with something challenging to do is a no-brainer. A natural hunter, your cat will enjoy hours of romping, biting, and playing with almost anything that resembles prey—and you know that if you don't provide her with something to investigate and paw at, she'll almost certainly make her own fun. The problem is that there's no guideline for what elements combine to make the perfect toy for a cat.

When I visit vendors at cat shows, they'll always rave about the toys their cats like to play with. "This is a great toy—my cat loves it and plays with it for hours," is often the statement I hear. So I purchase the new toy, take it home to my cat, and guess what happens? The packaging is often more interesting to her than the toy itself. That's because cats have different tastes and personalities. What works for one feline won't necessarily work for another. So you should resign yourself to the fact that you will end up investing (and wasting!) a bit of your time and money on trinkets your cat may never play with.

If there's good news about this, it's that cat toys are relatively inexpensive. Most fur mice, for instance, are a downright steal! If you go to a cat show and buy single toys from several vendors, you can usually get quite an assortment for very little money.

The overwhelming problem with toys is that your cat is quite intelligent and can get easily bored with the same toys day after day. That's why you need to rotate them frequently. The solution to this is to take several toys and bury them in a container containing catnip (to disguise the smell and make them fresh). Then, rotate them with the other toys about once a week. Provide several different types

How a cat acts depends a great deal on the overall environment in which she lives daily. Cats are basically homebodies—they like to stay in the comfort of their own territory.

of toys so that your cat has variety and plenty of mental stimulation.

Cat Trees

Cats are three-dimensional thinkers. In the wild, they climb trees to hunt and escape danger. Unfortunately, in today's household, we really don't give much thought to vertical spaces when it comes to a cat's needs—hence the value of cat trees.

Cat trees are more or less carpeted gyms that your kitty can climb to look down upon her kingdom in her regal manner (peasants!). She can also climb to safety when scared or when the family dog is pestering her. Most cats love being up high, and having a sturdy place to climb makes it all that much more inviting.

Many cat trees incorporate scratchers in rope, sisal, or even corrugated cardboard. Some incorporate toys, and while these may prove amusing, they shouldn't be relied on as your kitty's only source of entertainment.

You can get fairly basic to extravagant designs. If you're on a budget, you should be able to find a nice cat tree more inexpensively at a local pet-supply store or even from a mail-order, Internet, or catalog store. Custom-made

Toys, scratchers, and cat trees provide your cat with necessary stimulation and exercise.

cat trees can be ordered to match your decor with no problem, but these are bound to be pricier. Remember, the bigger they are and the more stuff you add, the higher the price.

If your cat doesn't show a lot of interest in the cat tree, try putting it in another location. Placing it near a window is always a good choice. Or try placing it near shelves where your kitty likes to climb. If she likes catnip, try sprinkling it around the tree. You can also use a tickler or lure toys to entice her onto this new piece of furniture. In no time, your cat will be enjoying her new digs.

Cat Scratchers

Scratching is a normal feline behavior. It's instinctive because cats use it to mark their territory, sharpen their claws, and even to get a good stretch. They need to scratch, but they shouldn't need to scratch your sofa. That's where cat scratchers come in.

There are many different shapes and sizes, but the best scratchers are obviously the ones your cat will like. Some are vertical, while others are horizontal. The best choices are the ones that provide a long stretch and a large scratching area made from appropriate materials. Made from all types of things, they can be cardboard, sisal, carpet, or soft wood—anything that allows your cat to scratch to her heart's content.

Many cat trees come with scratchers, but don't limit your cat to just one or two trees. She may need to scratch in the living room, bedroom, or your study. If she does, put a scratcher right by the objects she has been scratching to divert her attention to something other than your furniture.

Litter Boxes

Oddly enough, where you put your kitty's litter box is important. Cats have needs just like humans do, so it's important to put the litter box where your kitty can get to it easily. Otherwise, she will make her own litter box.

If you have more than one cat, it's also necessary to have several litter boxes.

Making Old Toys New

You can give new life to old toys by placing them in a container filled with catnip. After a week, pick up the toys your cat is currently playing with and replace them with the "new and improved" ones. I guarantee she'll think you went shopping for presents just for her. In the meantime, put the original toys in the catnip for a week so that you can continue to please your kitty with the enhanced substitutes.

You never know when a bully cat will play king of the roost, so providing one litter box per cat is important to prevent squabbling and to allow each pet comfortable access to her toilet areas.

You must also consider the type of litter box your cat needs to use. For example, big cats need big litter boxes and small cats need litter boxes that don't make them feel like they are climbing Mount Everest. Some felines get claustrophobic using covered litter boxes, while other cats love the privacy. Learn your cat's tastes and plan accordingly.

HOUSEHOLD HARMONY

Having the proper accessories to meet your cat's daily needs will not only ensure her overall happiness but her physical and mental well-being as well—not to mention that a content cat is more likely to be a well-adjusted companion.

If you ensure that your cat is comfortable, secure, and living in harmony with her natural instincts, she is more likely to be a well-adjusted companion.

House Rules

Your new cat will have a lot to learn when she moves in. In addition to figuring out where the litter box is, what time she can expect to be fed, and where to find the best bird-watching spot, she will have to learn the "rules" of the household.

Teach your pet what is and isn't acceptable in your home right from the start. Try to correct an unwanted behavior as soon as you notice it, because the longer it continues, the harder it will be to break your cat of the bad habit. In time and with enough reinforcement, your cat will learn what you expect of her.

Family members will also need to learn all the rules for cohabitating with a cat, which include responsible daily care as well as constant attention to keeping the house pet-proofed. The ultimate responsibility falls on you to make sure that your cat behaves and is well taken care of.

SO NOW YOU KNOW...

- Keeping your cat indoors is the safest option.
- If you must have an indoor/outdoor kitty, install a fence or enclosure to ensure her safety.
- Cats need and appreciate lots of new, interesting toys to play with throughout the day.
- Placement of cat trees, cat scratchers, and litter boxes is very important.
- How a cat acts depends a great deal on the overall environment in which she lives daily.

Despite what some people believe, you think that it's healthier for your cat to get some exercise and fresh air—to do what cats naturally do—rather than be cooped up in the house 24/7. But your cat has always been a bit of a tomcat. She yowls and screams, getting into fights with other cats.

Chapter 4

Cattin' Around: Rethinking the Outdoor Cat

She's been getting into the next-door neighbors' garbage and digging in their garden, wrecking everything. Another neighbor is mad because your feisty feline leaves dirty paw prints on his car. Your neighbors have had it.

It's hard to believe all the fuss being made over a little kitty. Not only that, but you've been warned that if animal control catches your pet, you'll be in for a whopping fine when you go to the shelter to retrieve her. Not good. Yet many of these behaviors are instinctual—they have been programmed into your cat by Mother Nature. You can't really expect to change them. Or can you?

RETHINKING CATS

As a responsible pet owner, you must think carefully about the many dangers your cat may face outside your home. Never allow her to roam unsupervised.

Until the twentieth century, cats were considered outdoor animals. During those earlier times, a majority of people lived in rural areas, so cats were mostly kept for rodent control and only occasionally thought of as pets. Also, because most cats relied on going outside to do their business, keeping a cat strictly indoors wasn't feasible. People didn't look at pets the way we do now.

That was then; this is now. Currently, more than 300 million people live in the United States, and few live in truly rural areas. The cat hasn't become obsolete, but she is no longer needed to do the job for which she was first domesticated. Although we may get vermin in our homes, we can take care of them with various commercial products. Instead, cats have become more popular than ever—even more popular than dogs—in their role as companion animals. As a cat owner, you should not be thinking of your cat in her former role but as a true companion who will be your friend for life.

The Modern Life of Cats

In this new century, our modern world is much more complex and crowded. As responsible pet owners, we must think carefully about the dangers that lie outside our homes. Cats aren't savvy about roads, highways, predators, dogs, or people who may mistreat them, which is why you shouldn't allow your cat to roam freely outdoors. Every year, thousands of cats, many wearing collars, end up killed. It breaks my heart to see these animals, with their little pink or blue collars, left lying on the side of the road. I wonder what their owners would think seeing them lying there or what they would tell their children, who will miss their precious pets terribly.

But road hazards aren't the only problem. I once spoke with a woman who wept because a dog had killed her cat right in the front yard. She was angry at the neighbors for letting their dog run loose, but I have often wondered why she didn't see the need to keep her cat inside before this tragedy occurred. What's more, dogs aren't the only predators, even in large cities. Foxes and coyotes now dwell in urban areas, and they have been known to prey on pets. And then there is the random person who will mistreat cats found wandering away from home. If that weren't enough, there is a host of incurable diseases such as feline immunodeficiency virus (FIV), also known as feline AIDS, and feline leukemia (FeLV) that your cat can contract if in contact with infected strays or their waste.

So with all these dangers lurking, why would anyone let his cat roam freely? There are various reasons, ranging from the belief that it's cruel to keep a cat inside to owners doing it because they've always done so. But maybe it's time to rethink that decision.

Why Cats Stray

While cats are indeed territorial, they can extend their range fairly far from home. And because there are no real boundaries you can set to keep your cat in a specified area (a regular fence won't do it), your cat is pretty much on her own when it comes to deciding where she wants to go. If she's intact, you can bet she's going to be looking for suitors when she is in heat (or if you have an intact male, he's going to be looking for females), so her range is naturally going to expand.

And even though your cat loves you and you love your cat, you've pretty much told her that she is free to go out into the world to play and explore far continents just by sending her outdoors unsupervised. But do you really expect a domestic cat to figure out what's safe and what's not in that complex urban jungle or the wilderness of unfamiliar yards? Would you allow a small child to roam freely? I didn't think so. So why do that to your beloved kitty?

It's true that some cats lead content lives staying close to home, but most find the freedom just too tempting, so they wander off and get into trouble. After all, there are plenty of interesting and exciting things to see and do "out there." If your cat is intact, she may be looking for a mate or maybe even a fight. She will be tempted by interesting smells such as garbage or that pile of compost near your neighbor's vegetable garden. In short, cats roam because they can—because you allow them to.

So how do you stop your cat from venturing out? The first solution is obvious. As discussed earlier, make your cat an inside-only cat. This is probably the most feasible solution for anyone who lives in an apartment and doesn't have access to a fenced-in backyard. An inside-only cat can be quite happy if there are enough activities to keep her occupied and entertained.

The second way is to fence in your backyard using special cat fencing, but even this has drawbacks. The reality is that even if you have a fenced-in backyard, your cat may still be able to get out, or worse yet, other animals may be able to get in. If you do decide to have a fenced-in backyard, do not rely on normal fencing to contain your cat. Cats can easily climb up or jump on even a 6-foot (1.8-m) fence, and most regular fences are no deterrent.

The best solution is to keep your cat indoors. Most cats who have been outdoor cats may be a bit resistant at first, but with attention from you and enough things to do, your cat will come to enjoy being inside.

If you permit your cat to spend time outdoors, use special cat fencing to keep her safe. Cats, as well as many of their predators, can easily climb up or jump most regular fences.

YOWLING

Outdoor cats have a tendency to be very loud. Females in season and tomcats "in the mood" can get pretty vocal when looking for mates. A cat will let others know that this is her territory through loud vocalizations. You may enjoy hearing your cat, but I'll bet your neighbors will get tired of it rather quickly.

But you can't train your cat not to yowl while she's outdoors. There's no such thing as an anti-yowl cat collar—and even if there were, your cat wouldn't get the point anyway. Throwing something at your cat only teaches her to avoid you; she doesn't understand that you want her to stop making noise. So you just have to deal with the consequences, which may not always be pleasant.

FIGHTING

If you've lived in any suburban or urban neighborhood long enough, I'm sure you've heard hissing and spitting from some pretty irate cats. Cats get into fights for many reasons, usually over territory or mates. They can be pretty loud and obnoxious, especially at 3 a.m.

But fighting is more than just obnoxious. Cats can spread disease such as feline leukemia and feline immunodeficiency virus through open wounds. Even kitty colds can be caught through association with other cats. And while you may think that your cat is immune to certain diseases because she had her vaccinations, the reality is that vaccinations sometimes fail and some diseases can't actually be vaccinated against. Do you really want to expose your cat to these health risks?

When it comes to fighting, the good news is you can avoid it altogether by keeping your cat inside. This is yet another reason to rethink your outdoor-kitty philosophy.

OVERPOPULATION

Unless you're a breeder who shows cats at one of the many cat shows every year, there's absolutely no reason to have intact cats. Intact cats aren't any more loving or sweet than neutered cats, and the reality is there are more than enough wonderful cats to go around. Just ask anyone who works at a shelter about "kitten season." Every spring and summer, dozens of kittens are brought into shelters, many who will never have homes. The problem is manyfold: A lot of people don't spay and neuter their cats, and when they venture outdoors, they will mate, producing litter after litter of kittens.

You see, a cat's biology isn't like ours or even like a dog's, for that matter. When cats mate, the act of mating actually causes the female to ovulate, thus guaranteeing pregnancy. Given the fact that cats can have several kittens each time they mate, it doesn't take long for their numbers to get out of control.

The best thing you can do is spay and neuter your cats if you haven't already.

Outdoor Health Hazards

Your cat can get very sick from fighting with other cats. Both feline leukemia (FeLV) and feline immunodeficiency virus (FIV) can be contracted by your cat when she is fighting through exposure to infected saliva, especially when scratched or bitten. Feline leukemia can further be spread through infected water bowls and cat-to-cat grooming. Both of these diseases are deadly and incurable.

They can be spayed and neutered as young as eight weeks of age, and any competent vet can perform this procedure safely. Your cat will be less prone to cattin' around and more focused on you. What's more, spaying and neutering helps prevent certain cancers associated with the reproductive organs. It prevents unwanted kittens, and it prolongs your cat's life. It's the right thing to do.

RETRAINING YOUR CAT TO BE AN INDOOR-ONLY CAT

So how on earth do you retrain your outdoor-loving cat to be an indoor-only cat? Basically, it all comes down to one thing: activity. A busy cat is a happy cat—inside or out. Plus, you can't ignore the benefits of providing your cat with lots to do. Regular exercise keeps your feline limber and strong. It strengthens and tones her muscles, keeps her at a proper weight, increases her energy level, and helps her sleep better. But equally important, exercise and play will fend off boredom, keep her mind sharp, and usually help prevent those pesky behavioral issues.

Managing the Transition

As a result of controlled living conditions, indoor cats live much longer and tend to be healthier in the long run.

Your challenge in retraining your outdoor cat is to provide enough indoor distractions to keep her as intrigued as she would be outdoors. Cat gyms and cat trees, toys filled with catnip, interactive toys, and other items are all designed to mimic her activity in the wild: climbing, perching, jumping, and hunting. For example, your cat will enjoy a perch or two at her favorite windows so that she can keep an eye on what's going on outside.

To prevent bad habits, you'll need to provide plenty of scratchers near areas your cat may normally scratch. You'll also need litter boxes filled with her favorite litter—keep them clean so that she will use them. Using calming pheromones is also very helpful to make the transition easier.

Despite these opportunities for activity, your cat may still yowl or demand to go outside. If this is the case, try distracting her with food and perhaps work with her using clicker training to teach her more appropriate behavior (see Chapter 2). Whatever you do, ignore her vocalizations, because if you

Low-Cost Spay and Neuter Services

Many national and local programs provide free or low-cost spay/neuter services. They usually work with local vets nationwide. When you contact them, they will put you in touch with a local low-cost program. Some participating organizations are:

SPAY/USA
(800) 248-SPAY
www.spayusa.org
SPAY USA has more than 950 sterilization programs and clinics nationwide, with approximately 8,000 veterinarians in their network. Rates vary by region and veterinarian.

Friends of Animals
(800) 321-PETS
www.friendsofanimals.org

When you contact Friends of Animals, you'll receive a list of participating veterinarians in your area. A fee is required (currently $65 for a female cat and $51 for a male cat) for each procedure. After mailing a check or purchasing a voucher online, the organization will send you a certificate that can be used for the service at any veterinary clinic on the list. There are no additional costs incurred.

react to her in any way, she's rewarded each time she meows. If she just won't stop meowing, try wiggling a teaser feather on the opposite side of the room. As she comes to it, click and treat to reinforce the new behavior (the cessation of the meowing), and play with her for a while.

Keep in mind that because your kitty isn't being quite as active as she would be outdoors, she may need to consume fewer calories. Talk with your veterinarian about putting her on an indoor diet. (Some foods are specially formulated for less active cats.) If your cat starts gaining weight, you may have to have your veterinarian evaluate her.

Outdoor Envy

Creatures of habit, cats can be resistant to change, especially when faced with giving up their outdoor meanderings. You may find yourself dealing with a clever escape artist. A cat who is used to going outdoors will often wait by the door, looking for an escape route. When opening any exterior doors, pick up your kitty so that she won't run out or simply keep her in another room with the door closed whenever there's a lot of traffic in and out of the house. If necessary, you can also purchase outdoor containment systems or enclosures so that your cat will be able to enjoy the outdoors safely.

Bonding Time

To make the indoor transition a success, spending quality time with your kitty— something you may not have done much before—is a must. Regular play sessions will help diffuse that pent-up energy and strengthen the bond between you and your feline companion.

Although sharing your home with a cat may pose challenges and will require you to take on new responsibilities, you will be an important part of her daily life. In return, she will give you loving affection and enjoyment for years to come.

SO NOW YOU KNOW...

- It's downright dangerous to let your cat roam.
- Your cat is better off as an indoor-only cat.
- Your cat should be spayed and neutered, not only to prevent unwanted pregnancy but for other health reasons as well.
- You *can* retrain an outdoor cat to be a happy indoor cat.

INDOOR ACTIVITY

Scheduling regular playtime and providing a variety of toys will keep an indoor cat entertained and happy. The best types of toys for your cat are the ones that allow you to interact with her. Not only will she get needed exercise and have fun, but playing together with them will enhance the bond that you share with your feline friend. These interactive toys include fishing pole types with feathers or mice attached to a string or the "ticklers" or "teasers" that have feathers or springy stuff on the end of a rod. The fishing pole and rod toys are designed so that you can keep your hands away from those sharp claws and teeth (very important!). What's more, by using these toys instead of your hands or feet, your cat will learn that your extremities are not toys.

Some interesting toys that cat experts have found to be useful include:

- battery-operated or spring-loaded toys
- catnip toys (these work only for adult cats and cats who have the "catnip gene")
- crinkly or glittery balls
- fishing toys
- food puzzle balls
- fur mice
- stuffed animals
- teaser toys

Cats are intelligent animals who need stimulation and interaction in their world. Those who do not get enough play or interaction with their owners can become bored, restless, and develop problem behaviors. Set aside 10 to 15 minutes every day to play with your feline friend. Your cat will look forward to your scheduled time together and will miss it if you skip a day. Play not only socializes your pet, but it's a great way to give her the exercise she needs while keeping her mind and instincts sharp.

Make sure that your cat has plenty of safe toys to play with. Leave the toys out when you're not home so that she can amuse herself during the day. Every so often, buy a new toy and introduce it to your cat, and then rotate out an old toy. She will find the new toy interesting, and in a few days you can bring back the old toy. Your cat will think that the "old" toy is new again.

You love your cat. You think she's, well, the cat's meow. But you've decided she's an indoor cat, and you may be wondering if she's lonely or if perhaps she would do better with a pal to keep her occupied. Keep in mind, though, that adding a second pet should be a decision you make because you want another pet, not because you want to get a playmate for your kitty.

Chapter 5

Two Isn't Necessarily Company: Adding Another Cat or Pet

Quite honestly, she may or may not like the company. The reality is that you won't really know whether she will tolerate a newcomer until you've introduced the pet to your household. And then, of course, it's too late.

Cats hate change, and by altering the status quo, you've gambled on the outcome. But the good news is that adding a new pet can often take place without a lot of fuss and bother. The trick is to make the introductions slowly and to work patiently with your cat to ensure that the transition is as smooth and unthreatening for her as possible.

CHOOSING THE NEWCOMER

When adding a pet to your household, try to choose one you think your cat will be happy to meet. That may seem obvious, but not all cats are the buddy type. So before you go off to the shelter to find that newcomer, keep your cat's temperament in mind—can she handle dealing with a stranger? Some cats may surprise you and adjust to a new companion in spite of being timid. On the other hand, many won't. You'll have to think carefully about what's best for your pet. After all, she'll probably spend more time with the new family member than you will.

You might want to hedge your bets by looking for a cat with a personality that is similar to that of your current cat. Is your cat laid-back and quiet, or is she rambunctious and playful? Based on her temperament, you will have a number of options. Kittens are usually tolerated well but may be too rambunctious for an older feline. A kitten or cat of the opposite sex might make things easier—or might not. A puppy might be a little much for your kitty to handle, but an adult dog will usually get along with cats. Of course, you would never want to choose an animal that your cat would think of as prey such as a bird or a hamster.

Top Cat

Cats can be solitary creatures by nature, and if your feline has been top cat for a long time, she may not like another feline invading her territory. That doesn't necessarily mean that you shouldn't get another cat—plenty of households have more than one. However, if your fur kid seems happy and content, keeping an "only pet" isn't necessarily a bad idea—especially if she gets lots of love and affection.

As you can see, there is no easy way to predict how your cat will react to a newcomer. Before making any final decisions, keep these general rules of thumb in mind:

- Younger animals are better tolerated by established pets.
- Getting two kittens at once is a good idea because they will grow up together and benefit from keeping each other company.
- If you adopt an older dog, your safest option is to choose one who is known to get along with cats.
- If your cat doesn't seem like the social type, it may be best to settle on giving her all of your love and attention while you have the privilege of sharing your home with her.

Adding Another Cat

Although your cat may take well to a new companion, you can improve your chances of a smooth transition by introducing a kitten or a spayed or neutered cat of the opposite sex. Mammals tend to be more tolerant of the opposite sex

You won't know whether your cat will tolerate a newcomer until you've introduced the pet to your household.

Do Your Homework

There are many dogs out there who get along splendidly with their feline family members, but raising a puppy and a kitten together is probably the best way to get them to live well together long term. Yet despite proper socialization and training, there still may be challenges. For example, some dogs from prey-driven breeds (like Northern breeds and sighthounds) may never be completely trustworthy with cats, even when they are raised with them. These breeds have a strong instinct to hunt and fight, and if your cat runs or taunts your dog, those behaviors could incite a chase with unpleasant consequences. Do your homework when choosing a companion for your kitty!

and to animals that are less of a dominance threat, but there's no guarantee. If you decide to introduce an older adult cat, try selecting one who has already interacted with other felines in a similar environment.

Be careful to avoid pedigreed cats that are naturally dominant. For example, Turkish Vans are very loveable to humans but can be bullies to other cats. When in doubt, learn more about pedigreed cats through the Cat Fanciers' Association (CFA) at www.cfa.org or The International Cat Association (TICA) at www.tica.org.

Once you've settled on the type of cat you want, whether pedigreed or mixed breed (also known as a moggie), start your search at a shelter or rescue. There are lots of wonderful homeless kitties just waiting for new families. Although you may not find as many pedigreed cats there as purebred dogs, you should still be able to locate a few after a bit of scouting around. Breed clubs often run rescues, too—their contact information is listed on the CFA and TICA websites. You can also look for a cat at Petfinder.com (www.petfinder.com). If you *must* purchase a pedigreed cat from a breeder, I highly recommend that you read my book, *Bring Me Home! Cats Make Great Pets,* to learn how to find a reputable breeder. (See Resources.)

Before making your final choice, ask the rescue or shelter workers if the particular cat you are interested in is good with other cats. In many cases they can tell you if she has had positive or negative interactions with other shelter cats. If they can't, you'll have to trust your instincts on that individual's personality.

Cats behave differently in shelter environments than they would at home because they're under a lot of stress. Even so, you should consider the shelter workers' evaluation of the cat's temperament a guide to help you make your decision.

Adding a Dog

Yes, cats and dogs can live together peacefully in the same household. Your cat may enjoy the company of another species—in this case, a dog—provided that he already knows the rules about not

You can improve your chances of a smooth transition by introducing a kitten or a spayed or neutered cat of the opposite sex.

antagonizing the other pets. However, as mentioned earlier, there are caveats to this general rule. Sighthounds (like Greyhounds, Whippets, Salukis) and Northern breeds (like Alaskan Malamutes and Siberian Huskies) are probably not good dogs to add to a family that has cats. While there are exceptions, these dogs have strong prey drives and are therefore more likely to chase, hunt, and even kill a cat. For similar reasons, even some terriers may not be suited to being cat buddies. This all will depend largely on the temperament of the dog and whether he will be raised with the cat.

When looking at a particular breed of dog to add to your family, consider one that will be a calm family dog. Not all breeds have the same characteristics, so don't be lured into getting a particular breed because you like the look of the dog or because that breed is popular. Get the facts. You'll need to make an informed decision that will affect your cat and your life for 10 to 15 years.

You can learn about the different breeds on the American Kennel Club's (AKC) website at www.akc.org, but you'll find out even more about a specific breed if you visit the breed club's website. Most clubs offer detailed online information about their breed. (Contact information is listed on the AKC's website.)

Contacting breeders, handlers, and owners within the breed club should be your next step when deciding on a particular breed. Most breed club members will be brutally honest when it comes to their dogs' ability to get along with cats. It's wise to listen to the advice given by the people who breed and show these dogs. If they tell you their breed does not do well with cats, take their input to heart and look elsewhere.

Once you've settled on a particular breed, you can visit a breeder. You should also consider going to a shelter or looking on Petfinder.com (www.petfinder.com) to find your perfect pet. You may be surprised to learn that many dogs in shelters or rescues are purebred—and some are even puppies.

Choosing a dog who will fit in with your family won't be too difficult if you've done your homework. Of course, professional breeders will be very informative and helpful during your selection process. Again, in many cases the people at the shelter or rescue can tell you if the dog you are interested in is an appropriate companion for a cat or if there is another dog who is better suited for your family and home environment. If they can't, you'll have to trust the breed research you've done as well as your own instincts.

Like cats, dogs behave differently in shelter environments, so accept the shelter worker's evaluation of the dog's personality as a guide. It really does depend on you, your cat, and of course, your preferences.

Cats and dogs can live together peacefully in the same household. When looking at a particular breed of dog to add to your family, consider one that will be a calm family dog.

Adding Small Pets

If you decide that the next pet you want isn't a dog or another cat but something smaller, you may want to rethink that choice. Small pets such as rodents, small lizards, and fish may provide hours of entertainment for your cat, but the stress of being hunted by a larger predator will eventually kill them.

If you do decide to get smaller "pocket pets," keep them away from your cat at all times. Remember, cats can easily climb to get to the things they want, so simply putting the animal's cage on a high shelf isn't enough. Your pocket pet must stay in a safe, stress-free environment in a location that won't allow your cat to antagonize him. No matter what kind of pet you choose to bring home, always provide him with a secure environment.

MAKING INTRODUCTIONS

Bringing a new pet into your household can be a very stressful time for your cat, which is why you need to do some planning beforehand. Most people try to force the situation on their established pet by putting the newcomer in her territory right away, which can end in total disaster. Your kitty could react negatively to the newcomer, or the newcomer may try to chase your kitty every chance he gets. First impressions are crucial, so you'll have to start slowly and get your pets used to each other before you introduce them to living together unsupervised in your home.

Introducing a Dog

The reality is that pet owners want things to happen quickly so that they can get their household back to normal as soon as possible. This is understandable but not practical when dealing with pets, especially dogs and cats together. Animals have their own timelines, and the adjustments you may think should only take a few days or a week may actually require several weeks to a few months.

In the best-case scenario, your dog and cat will think nothing of each other—and may even like each other—and life will go back to normal quickly. But that doesn't always happen, especially if your cat has never dealt with dogs or your dog is interested in "inviting your cat to dinner."

Keep Them Separated!

Because throwing together two animals that don't know each other or that may initially dislike each other usually won't work—and will likely cause even more problems—you're going to have to figure out how to keep them separated while they get used to their new situation. This will require you to look at the floor plan of your home to come up with a solution with which both pets and humans can comfortably live.

First, set aside a room or two for your new dog. (If he is a puppy, you'll thank me later if he isn't housetrained yet!) Choose an area that prevents your dog or puppy from having access to your cat. This place should also ideally be near the door so that you can take your dog or puppy outside to do his business in a quick fashion.

In the meantime, make sure that the area in which you are keeping your cat contains everything she needs: food, water, scratchers, and of course, a litter box. It won't do any good to have her go through the "rooms of terror" just to do her business. Use those pheromone sprays or plug-ins to maintain a calming atmosphere for her. There are calming pheromones for dogs as well, but those take time to work—as long as six weeks—so you may want to plan ahead and plug those in as soon as you know you're getting a dog.

The next step is to have the pets investigate each other's rooms without having

Introduce new pets to your cat slowly so that they have time to get to know each other and get used to each others' scent, sounds, and activities.

the other animal present. Having them spend a few days in each area is probably a good idea because it gets them used each other's scent. (You may wish to move the cat's things into the room where the dog is kept and vice versa.)

The reason behind keeping your dog and cat separated is very simple: Both are getting used to each other's scent, sounds, and activities. This is the lowest stress option you have when dealing with the initial introduction of your new pet into the home.

Provide an Escape Route

Before you decide to make the big introduction, reevaluate your cat's escape routes. She needs to be able to climb to safety to avoid your dog's inquisitive nose, so every room in your house should provide her with a way she can quickly flee if he frightens her or chases her. Large cat trees, vertical furniture, and even cat steps are useful to prevent her from being bugged too much. Some domestic cats don't necessarily think of climbing as a means of escape, but you can train your kitty to do this by teaching her where these "vertical safety zones" are in each room.

First, choose an item on which your cat can practice climbing, such as a cat tree. Begin the exercise by flicking a teaser toy back and forth until she's interested in it. As she goes for the teaser, flick it again and continue doing so while gradually leading her closer to the cat tree. When she finally arrives at the base of the vertical safety zone, in this case the cat tree, bring the teaser toy up to the first level she can climb. You may have to work with her a bit to get her there, but once you do, play with her to reinforce her choice. Continue playing with the teaser until you get her to climb to the top of the cat tree. If the jump to any of the levels is too hard, your cat may not wish to go farther. If she is not high enough to ensure her safety, reevaluate the escape route plan and choose something that is a little easier for her to climb.

Dog, Meet Cat

Your cat and dog don't seem to be very concerned about each other's presence. Escape routes are available in each room. You think it's time to start the actual face-to-face introductions. Good.

There are several ways to proceed, but the best way to start is to set up a baby gate in the doorway of your dog's room. It should be tall enough and sturdy enough to keep your dog contained. Test this by keeping the gate in place for a few days to see if he can get out.

Make the initial introduction when your dog is tired, usually after he has exercised and after he has eaten. With your dog still contained in the gated room, allow your cat out of her area so that she can approach the dog if she'd like. Be sure that she can easily retreat to another part of the house if she becomes anxious. At this point, it's up to her to investigate this strange new creature. If your dog starts barking or trying to get through the gate, correct him immediately. (You can use clicker training to focus his attention on you instead of the cat. I cover clicker training and dogs in *The Simple Guide to Getting Active with Your Dog*. See Resources.) Interest in the cat is okay, but barking and aggressive behavior are not.

If the first introduction isn't going well, return your cat to her private area and try working with your dog on basic commands for a few days. You want your dog to be able to ignore your cat or at least only show mild interest in her. Once you feel a bit more confident that he can behave appropriately, let your cat out again. If she doesn't want to visit yet, that's okay. She may need some time to retest the waters. Leave the gated door in place, and let her approach the dog on her own terms. The ideal situation is that your cat feels she has the run of the house and can visit with him whenever she feels like it without feeling pressured or fearful. Of course, your dog may not be pleased, but this is only a temporary arrangement.

If you can't accommodate this type of setup in your home or apartment, you can put your dog in a travel crate for a brief time and let the cat approach him when she is ready. This isn't quite as ideal because the dog can get stressed about being enclosed in one place, and he won't be comfortable not being able to meet the cat on his own terms. Both conditions may also cause your dog to pound at the crate to get out, which won't be helpful. Only do this for a short period each day until both animals are calm in each other's presence.

As a final option, you can plan a face-to-face introduction in which your dog is kept on a leash while your cat is allowed to be at liberty in the same room. Again, she will approach the dog when she is ready. Correct your dog for any wild behavior, especially for leaping at the cat. You can also use clicker training to distract your dog whenever the cat is in the room and

Safe Introductions

You may be wondering how long it's necessary to keep your pets separated before introducing them safely to each other. The truth is that it can often take more time than you'd expect. You have to watch both pets for signs that they've adjusted to each other's scent and sounds. The indication that things have become more civil is that each pet is relaxed and only casually interested in the other. But this can sometimes take several days to several weeks, depending on the individuals concerned and the overall size of the shared living space.

People tend to rush introductions when they shouldn't. Remember that *you* know all about the new pet, but your current pet does not. You're asking for a change in the status quo, which for cats is always a big deal. Be patient. In the long run, you'll achieve the best outcome for all concerned.

have him focus on you instead of on her. After a few sessions, you'll get to work with your dog off leash, and eventually, you won't need to use the clicker at all.

How long does this take? It depends largely on the reactions of your dog and cat to one another. Some owners are able to introduce on-leash fairly quickly and go to off-leash without much fuss (with maybe an occasional correction for showing too much interest). Other pets take a long time to form what becomes an uneasy truce.

When It's Not Working Out

You've tried everything to get your cat and dog to be best buddies, but you've failed. It's been months, but the dog still isn't interested in sharing his home or family with her, and he isn't able to just ignore her. What do you do?

Believe it or not, the situation isn't hopeless yet. Many dogs and cats can live together with more effective training. You may have to admit to yourself that perhaps you're just not doing it right and that you may need a little help to get some sanity back into your life.

Your best bet in this case is to locate and consult a dog behaviorist or trainer who is willing to work with you and your dog. These professionals will often come to your home and assess the problem immediately and then recommend workable solutions

When adding a new dog to your family, be certain your cat can quickly flee if he frightens or chases her. Large cat trees, vertical furniture, and even cat steps are useful to prevent her from being bugged too much.

tailored to your needs. The International Association of Animal Behavior Consultants (IAABC, www.iaabc.org) and the trainers at the Association of Pet Dog Trainers (APDT, www.apdt.com) can provide you with contact information for professionals in your area.

Trainers and behaviorists can work wonders, even when you think that the situation is impossible. However, they're not miracle workers, and some dogs will never be trustworthy with cats no matter what you do. Then what? In these cases, you will have to commit to being vigilant in monitoring your pets at all times and supervising them whenever they are in the same space together. Your cat's basic nature will help keep the peace because she will avoid risking conflict. Also, keeping your cat and dog permanently separated can be a viable option for any household because adult cats tend to sleep 16 to 20 hours a day. You'll still need to maintain cat-only and dog-only areas in your house and allow each pet out at different times. More importantly, you will need to spend quality time with each of them to ensure their happiness and sense of security. Despite common misconceptions, both dogs and cats need regular daily attention from you, especially if they don't have buddies to hang around with. Although your cat is more of an independent creature, don't shortchange her on the time you spend with her. Even allowing her to sleep with you will provide bonding time she will appreciate.

Keep cats separated before introducing them to each other face to face. By proceeding slowly, you'll prevent many adjustment problems.

Introducing Another Cat

Some studies have shown that cats prefer to live in a single-cat household. While this may be the case, many people prefer to have more than one cat. If this is your choice, be prepared to make introductions properly.

Like introducing a dog, introducing a new cat to your established cat must be done in small steps. It takes a while for most felines to sort things out. Your cat may make friends with the newcomer right away, and they may fast become best buddies. That's the best-case scenario. Or your "queen of her domain" may not take a liking to the new cat and may simply ignore her. That's all right, too. The problem begins when one or both of your cats feel stressed and defend their territories either by urinating or scratching, or worse, by fighting with each other—not a win-win situation. By proceeding slowly, you'll prevent many of these problems.

Keep Them Separated!

Similar to introducing dogs, you will need to keep the two cats separated before introducing them to each other face to face. Before you start the process, apply feline pheromones (diffuser and spray) throughout the house and in the rooms where each cat will be kept. This will help reduce their anxiety about being in a new place, as well as aid in curbing unwanted behavior by keeping them calm.

Next, set aside a room for the new cat; a spare bedroom or bathroom works well. She will need to have her own litter box, scratcher, bed, and of course, food and water dishes. By doing this, your current cat will still have the run of most of the house but will smell the newcomer without the stress of having to deal with her actual presence within her territory, which she may fiercely protect.

Again, after a week or two of this, your cats shouldn't show any serious signs of stress. If they do, the separation should continue until they are relaxed with the new circumstances. The next step, as you might guess, is to have the cats investigate each other's areas for a few days without having the other individual present so that they can get used to each other's scent. Once both kitties appear to accept their new digs, you are ready for the meet and greet.

Cat, Meet Cat

During the time spent in each other's areas, your cats didn't seem to be too concerned about the apparent prior presence of the other feline they sniffed out. There are also no signs of territorial marking or clawing. You think it's time to begin actual face-to-face introductions.

There are several ways to do this, and all are viable. The first option is to put the newcomer in a large enclosure (a crate made for a dog works very well) and then let your other cat come into the room to investigate the newcomer. This gives your new cat a sense of security but allows the established cat to meet the newcomer on her own terms. After a few sessions without any serious

Play Training for Confidence

You can use play-training exercises to increase a victim cat's confidence and to bolster her status. Start by getting her interested in a teaser toy or a toy on a fishing line. Have her play with it freely at first. Next, let her catch it, even if her initial attempts aren't very skillful. Gradually encourage her to work harder to accomplish the goal of "capturing her prey."

By persuading your bullied cat to react naturally to something that won't harm her, such as a toy during a play session, and enticing her to follow her instincts by chasing after it and catching it, you will reinforce her confidence by allowing her to be proactive and aggressive. Aside from helping her sharpen her skills, this exercise also gives her quality time with you, which is a bonding experience that will make her feel more secure.

incidents, your two cats may be ready to meet without the crate.

Another option is to gate off a room as you were instructed to do in the section on introducing a new dog. Allow your established cat free access to the gated room so that she can approach the newcomer if she'd like. At this point, it's up to her to visit whenever the mood strikes. Again, if your cat doesn't want to visit, that's okay. Let her approach on her own terms. The problem with the gate scenario, however, is that a cat can jump the gate if she really wants to, so you won't be able to let her have free reign of the house. Plan these sessions only when you can supervise the entire encounter. Eventually, the two cats will become accustomed to one another so that you can proceed to a face-to-face introduction.

What's Mine Is Mine—Not!

When introducing one cat to another, keep in mind that a dominant cat may try to bully the more passive one. She may decide that her competitor is fair prey and attack her whenever she gets the chance. If you have an aggressive cat who won't play nicely, do the following:

- Provide more than one litter box, and keep them far enough apart so that one cat can't intimidate the other by preventing her from having access to a bathroom area.
- Provide enough food and water dishes in separate areas of the house so that there's no need for resource guarding.
- Allow the nonaggressor to roam the house while keeping the aggressor in a smaller area.
- Work on "building up" the nonaggressor's confidence through play training.
- Work on the "bully" cat's bad behavior by correcting inappropriate responses right away and positively reinforcing appropriate behavior.

Be aware that this dominance aggression can take some time to resolve (months, not days), so you may wish to consult a feline behaviorist for a more timely resolution.

When It's Not Working Out

Your cats are ready to spit nails. They're screaming and attacking each other, and you have mounting vet bills. You'll never have peace at this rate. What do you do?

Keeping your cats separated for long periods may make all

the difference between fighting and calm acceptance. Regular use of feline pheromones will also help ease a tense situation. Eventually, you may want to try allowing your cats to live together again, but do only under the guidance of a behaviorist, who will most likely recommend play training and other activities that will teach them to behave and get along better.

Despite all your efforts, your cats may simply tolerate each other and never really grow to like one another. That should be fine; as long as they don't fight, there can be harmony in the house. Just don't plan to add another cat anytime soon.

SO NOW YOU KNOW...

- Whether you introduce a new dog or another cat, the introductions must take place slowly and may take several weeks.
- To begin the process of introducing two pets, your best option is to keep your established cat and the newcomer separated. This gives both animals a chance to get used to each other's scent, sounds, and activities before they have to meet face to face.
- Once both pets are used to each other's presence while in separate rooms, you can begin face-to-face introductions using a gate as a protective barrier between them. This allows your established cat to get used to the stranger on her own terms while allowing the newcomer to feel safe.
- If your two pets can't seem to get along without antagonizing each other, consult a behaviorist. If the behaviorist can't help, you can still keep both pets happy by keeping them separated at all times.
- Not all dog breeds are good with cats. You'll need to check out the AKC's website at www.akc.org for information on potential breeds you're interested in before making a firm decision. You'll also need to consult with breeders or rescues workers to make sure that the individual you are interested in is likely to get along with cats.

If your two pets can't seem to get along without antagonizing each other, consult a behaviorist.

Chapter 6

Aggressive Behaviors: The Antisocial Cat

Many cats are loving and sweet. They enjoy being petted and love crawling up into your lap. They're friendly, and they greet people enthusiastically. What? Not your kitty? It's true. Some cats do live up to their rather aloof reputations. These "antisocial" cats can be downright aggressive, attacking people who walk by their yard or enter their house.

And forget about petting them—one pat may elicit a bite or a swipe of the claws. For their small size, these strong-willed cats pack quite a wallop. And while we often chuckle at the antics of feisty felines, it's no laughing matter if you're the one who ends up at the doctor's office getting several stitches.

The only way to effectively deal with this appalling conduct is to understand what causes aggressive behaviors, what these various rude behaviors mean, and what you can do to change them.

HELP! MY CAT HATES ME!

What do you do if your cat hates you? I mean, *truly* hates you. You wake up in the morning to find her pouncing on you with claws fully extended, or she takes a swipe at your feet whenever you walk by her. Is your situation completely hopeless?

Although there are some impossible cases, they are far and few between. While some abandoned cats have become feral and untrainable, domesticated animals have been raised around people, either by breeders or owners, so there's a good chance you can work out these aggressive problems with some time and patience.

Now, it's worth noting that some aggressive cats are born and not made (just as some aggressive dogs are born and not made). However, the majority of aggressive cats develop unwanted behaviors for various reasons, such as they are overstimulated, lack socialization, or are suffering from a painful condition. Although there aren't many quick fixes, there are effective ways to replace aggression with more positive behaviors.

TYPES OF FELINE AGGRESSION

Part of understanding your cat's aggression is understanding what triggers it. Treatment options will depend largely on the underlying root of the problem that is causing your cat to become aggressive rather than on the specific unwanted behaviors that result from it. Let's look at various types of aggression in more detail.

Play/Prey Aggression

Play/prey aggression is caused by the overwhelming desire to hunt something, whether it's the mouse that crawls along the baseboards, a feather teaser toy, or your foot. Cats are naturally

DID YOU KNOW?

Declawing a cat can lead to aggressive behavior. That's because the pain and anxiety caused by having lost part of the toes can last far longer than a few weeks or months after the operation. Think about how grouchy you may have felt when you've suffered pain that lasted longer than a few days. That's how a cat who has been declawed feels every day of her life because she's no longer equipped to deal with her environment in a comfortable way.

But there is hope. You can work with a behaviorist and your veterinarian if you suspect that part of your cat's aggression is due to being declawed. Medication can be prescribed to reduce the pain and/or the aggressive impulses, and the behaviorist can work with you and your pet to help you establish a better bond.

wired to chase after things, and seeing a feather or something that moves in a jerky fashion naturally incites this behavior.

This kind of aggression can also be encouraged by using your hands and feet to play with your cat. Doing so quickly identifies you as possible prey, and you therefore become the target of aggression.

Redirecting Play/Prey Aggression

Cats cannot ignore their instinct to hunt prey. Those who attack your hands and feet have, in a sense, been taught early on that hands and feet are easy targets because you've probably used them to engage your cat during play. This is why it's important to always use a toy, such as a teaser toy that is on a stick or a fishing pole, to redirect the aggression away from your fingers and toes. But of course, this won't help if your cat is already hunting them.

Training for this problem will require you to plan accordingly. You'll have to have teaser toys stationed throughout the house, ready to go if your cat attacks. Let's say you're walking into the kitchen and your cat darts out to grab your feet. Stand still and grab a teaser toy. Flick the teaser toy back and forth *away* from your body, and allow her to play with that instead. By standing still, you've made

Many aggressive cats develop unwanted behaviors because they are overstimulated, lack socialization, or are suffering from a painful physical condition.

yourself less of a target, and by focusing your cat on a teaser toy, you've interested her in the toy—a more exciting substitute.

You'll also want to institute regular playtime with your cat. By bonding with her and playing with her in the correct fashion, she'll start looking at you more as a friend and less as a pouncing target.

Sexual Aggression

Sexual aggression occurs between cats who wish to mate or between cats who are fighting over a mate. You won't see sexual aggression in neutered cats. Basically, this type of aggression occurs when one cat is fighting off another suitor or when a cat doesn't want to be mated by the individual making advances. This is clearly cat-on-cat aggression.

Stopping Sexual Aggression

The way to stop sexual aggression and eliminate other unwanted behaviors associated with it is to spay and neuter your frisky felines. However, for this to be completely effective, it is necessary for all cats in the household to be spayed/neutered to stop the various aggressive actions. Once you neuter all your pets, you can then slowly reintroduce them to each other.

Territorial Aggression

Territorial aggression sometimes occurs when cats feel that they must fiercely protect their territory. Occasionally, these territorial terrorists have even made the news with their extreme antics while chasing other creatures away from their yard—one cat recently featured actually chased a big black bear up a tree.

This type of aggression, however, isn't a laughing matter when it comes to visiting friends or neighbors, especially children, seniors, or unsuspecting strangers passing by your house. One owner in the UK was actually cited for having a vicious cat.

Fixing Territorial Aggression

Surprisingly, cats can become pretty territorial when it comes to their home. When dealing with a feline who is ready to fight tooth and claw over her abode, you may be wondering if you'll ever have visitors again.

Your first priority in this situation is to be aware that your cat is feeling pretty worried about protecting her home from other individuals (animal and human) who may be treading on her turf. If your cat is an indoor/outdoor cat, bring her indoors to limit her contact with strays and strangers.

Once indoors, you can use calming pheromones such as Feliway or Comfort Zone so that your kitty has comforting scents around her instead of the scent of that alley cat lurking outside the window. Outdoors, you may wish to use cat repellant to keep stray cats from visiting and spraying the area, thus causing more fear.

But just because your kitty can't interact with these strays doesn't mean that there won't be a problem. Just seeing a strange cat may cause her to behave in a frightened manner. Use shutters or blinds to eliminate the view from any windows that enable your cat to look out over high-traffic areas, and find a better window for her to sit and sun herself where the bothersome intruders won't show up. If you have more than one indoor cat and they are all getting grouchy with one another because of the strays, try separating them and reintroducing them with plenty of calming pheromones to go around.

When it comes to visitor envy, if your cat continues to be nasty toward friends or other unfamiliar people who come into your home after being properly introduced, you'll probably have to work with a behaviorist to be sure that it's territorial. One of the primary causes for this type of aggression is that your cat is feeling threatened because these guests are often trying to pet or play with her when she'd rather be left alone. Your cat is already on the defensive, so she may become a grouch in no time. A behaviorist can help work with you and your cat to

Aggression Reducers

There are a few items on the market that may help you manage an aggressive cat. Feliway and Comfort Zone with Feliway work exceptionally well in this regard. These products contain facial pheromones that give off a calming scent to cats. Because the smell is soothing and reassuring to your cat, she won't feel the need to behave in a territorial manner. If sprayed on areas that provoke aggressive tendencies, such as doors and windows, you may prevent possible altercations. You may also opt to use a diffuser, which will continuously disperse pheromones into the air throughout the house. By the way, this scent is undetectable to humans.

Although the makers of Feliway do not make any claims regarding this product and its use in treating aggression, it's my belief that cats exposed to it calm down considerably and are therefore less likely to be ill behaved.

get her on the right track; he'll analyze the possible triggers for territorial aggression and recommend the most effective ways to combat it given your circumstances.

Overstimulation

This is a scenario you have more than likely experienced at one time or another, often while you are having a bonding moment with your cat and showing her affection. For example, your cat may have come over to you for petting, and while you are complying, she whaps you with her claws or bites you really hard. You're left scarred and your cat is angry. What's going on?

Stopping the Attack During Petting Sessions

Overstimulation often occurs when your cat becomes riled up because—if you can believe this—there's too much petting. Independent by nature, most cats don't want to be petted or held for long periods. This isn't necessarily her problem, per se—it's yours. Your cat may only be able to tolerate a few rubs or may not want any. It depends on her mood. But don't get me wrong—if your cat hops into your lap or brushes up against you for a pet, you should oblige her. You just need to learn what the signs of overstimulation are and know how to avoid the repercussions.

Redirected aggression occurs because your cat can't quite show her anger or irritation toward another creature, so she bites or scratches the next best thing—you.

Signs that your cat is becoming overstimulated include ears flattening, pupils dilating, body stiffening, fur moving like a shiver across the body, tail lashing back and forth, and of course, a low growl. If your cat shows any of these signs, stop petting her. If necessary, move her off your lap. The idea is to react to these hints by removing the perceived threat so that your cat doesn't feel the need to demonstrate her displeasure. That way, she knows that she can give you the signals that say "Hey, stop petting me" before she has to do something rude. Solutions such as these increase the level of communication you share with your feline companion and will therefore strengthen the bond you share.

Redirected Aggression

Redirected aggression occurs because your cat can't quite show her anger or irritation toward another creature. As a result, she turns on you and bites or scratches the next best thing. For example, your kitty sees cats invading her territory outside, but she can't shoo them away from her distant domain. When you come around, she tests her "cathood" by scratching at you; after all, you *are* passing through her indoor territory. Not very nice, is it?

Redirecting Redirected Aggression

Anticipating redirected aggression is somewhat like looking into a crystal ball. Unless you can get a good look into the future, chances are it's pretty tough to determine what's going to cause your cat to become aggressive.

Once your cat shows redirected aggression, the best thing to do is to provide a distraction right after it happens. Use calming pheromones and play to diffuse the situation. Otherwise, the problem may get worse, not better. Also, if you can watch your cat closely and identify the situations that cause the aggressive behavior, you may be able to stop it from happening again. If the aggression continues and you are stumped, getting a cat behaviorist involved will help identify and eliminate the unwanted behaviors.

Fear/Pain Aggression

Fear and pain are basic natural aggressions, meaning that a preservation instinct is at the root of the aggressive behavior. The cat is sure she is in danger (and maybe she is) or is in such pain that her need to ensure survival has kicked in. Fear (I'm terrified of what's happening) or pain (I hurt so badly that I just want to get out of here and will do whatever it takes to do so) will cause a cat to become very forceful and uncompromising. Cats who suffer from either pain or fear aren't rational when it comes to their behavioral responses.

Pain aggression may or may not be obvious. For example, you know your cat is in pain if you accidentally step on her foot. But you may not be aware that she's in pain because of arthritis or some other biological problem. Cats don't handle discomfort well, and they don't often internalize it. They will lash out—and you may just be the closest fall guy. So even if you're pretty sure that the aggression is completely behavioral, have your vet examine your cat just to be sure.

Bullies

There's another type of aggression worth talking about, and that's the bad behavior of a bully cat. Maybe you know a bully cat. Bully cats aren't common, but when you meet them, they do make an impression. These cats can be bullies toward other cats, dogs, or even toward their humans.

Bullies are mostly demanding cats—if they don't get what they want, watch out! And they usually pack a wallop. They seem to have multiple personalities, so you never know what to expect. They demand lots of your time and attention, and if they don't get it, they nag or even become aggressive. They often show numerous aggressive behaviors that create conflict with their human family and visiting friends.

In a nutshell, these brazen bullies won't let their owners lead normal lives. Like the so-called dominant alphas of dogdom, these cats are the bad-girl kitties of the cat world. It may sound funny, but it's not. This can be a real problem, especially if you're a conscientious pet owner who really wants to do right by your pet. If you have a bully cat, you may feel that you're wrapped around your kitty's claw. For instance, she may decide that she wants to be fed right now and will meow constantly or claw you if you're not responding soon enough. She may hate strangers and attack them from behind. Your dog may even be intimidated and may try to avoid her whenever she's in a bossy mood.

Bully cats are not always born that way. Cats who are weaned too early from their mothers may become bullies, but more often it's the owner who creates the problem. Basically, you've created what amounts to a spoiled kid, and you have to correct this before it's too late.

First, go to your veterinarian and have your cat thoroughly examined. Medical conditions can often cause behavioral problems, so don't rule that out. Seeing an animal behaviorist is a good idea as well.

Handling a dominant cat need not be rocket science. It takes a lot of energy to behave badly, so if you diffuse some of that energy, you'll probably have a more content cat. Exercising your cat by providing her with interesting toys, cat trees, and play areas, in addition to playing with her, will help reduce the need to bully.

Don't Be a Tease: Redirected Aggression

If you rile up your cat during play sessions and then try to pet her immediately afterward, you are just asking for trouble. Your cat's rude behavior is probably due to overstimulation or redirected aggression because you just took away her favorite toy and she's not ready to release you from your obligation to entertain her!

If this happens often, the best thing to use when playing with your demanding cat is a teaser or a fishing toy. This way, you can avoid having your hands or feet hurt, and your cat can tell you she's finished playing by walking away when she gets bored. If you want to finish a session early, give her some toys to play with on her own, but don't expect to spend snuggle time with her now that she's in swat-and-pounce mode. It's a sure way of getting scratched or bitten.

Institute a "nothing in life is free" program. Instead of using their brains for good purposes, these bratty cats are like smart kids who like getting into trouble—so direct their intelligence toward positive tasks. Most cats are quite capable of learning tricks if they are working for some sort of reward. Start training your clever cat by teaching her a simple trick like "sit," and make her do it before she is fed or before giving her a toy. Teaching a cat to perform tricks to get what she wants distracts her from getting into trouble and redirects her toward a more positive behavior. Having a cat swatting you for food isn't fun; having a cat who will sit up and raise a paw is much more agreeable.

HOW TO PREVENT AGGRESSIVE BEHAVIOR

Your cat is aggressive. Maybe you've identified the type of aggression—maybe not. Maybe you're pretty sure that it's behavioral. There are several ways to work with your aggressive feline. A good first step is to look for a behaviorist who can evaluate your cat and propose solutions. Once the possible causes of your feisty feline's behavior have been determined, you can begin to implement those

Bullies are usually dominant cats who insist on getting lots of your time and attention—and if they don't get it, they will nag or become aggressive.

solutions at home. If you decide that you would rather try to tackle this yourself before seeking professional help, include the following in your kitty rehab program.

Spaying/Neutering

Before you begin any behavioral program, spay and neuter any cats in the household to prevent sexual tension. By eliminating the cause of sexual tension, you've eliminated sexual aggression, plus other unwanted behaviors. For example, although spaying and neutering may not eliminate spraying in the house, it should curtail it for the most part.

Spaying (removing the female cat's ovaries and uterus) and neutering (removing the male cat's testicles) are routine procedures that can be performed by any competent veterinarian. Kittens as young as eight weeks of age can be spayed or neutered with no detrimental effects.

Besides the obvious benefit of preventing unwanted pregnancies, spaying and neutering can also reduce or eliminate certain types of cancers in cats. All pet cats should be spayed and neutered for these reasons.

Playtime

Many cats become aggressive because they have too much pent-up energy.

Like the teenager who has nothing to do, bored and frustrated cats start channeling their energy into things they shouldn't. By playing with your cat several times a day, you give her an outlet for that energy and create a lasting bond with her as a result.

Types of Toys

When most people think of cat toys, they think about little fur mice or bags filled with catnip. The reality is that those are fine toys for your cat to play with on her own, but they aren't good to use when you play together. One reason for this is that you can accidentally get scratched when trying to grab the toy. More importantly, this can promote aggression because your cat will look at your hands as part of the toy. Ouch! The good news is that there are toys you can buy or make that allow you to safely interact with your cat.

Toys on long poles (commonly called teaser toys) and toys on fishing lines (called fishing toys) are excellent choices. These types of toys will keep your hands and feet safe from your kitty's claws while still providing hours of satisfying fun for your cat. You may be wondering about those battery-operated toys or toys that run on a track with which your kitty can play by herself. That isn't the point of the exercise here, and even if it were, some cats think that they're boring or scary. And even if your cat enjoys these toys, playing isn't just about wearing your cat down. It's also about bonding. By playing with your cat, you're building a positive bond with her.

It may take a bit of time and effort to determine which toys are best, but cat toys are fairly inexpensive, so you can experiment. Some fishing toys are actually set up so that you can easily replace the object at the end of the fishing pole (which also allows you to replaced a mangled toy). Some old standbys include feathers, Mylar ribbons, and fur or leather tassels, but the best toys are always the ones your cat likes. Just as with people, every cat has different tastes, so don't be afraid to try different things. If your cat finds a particular toy boring, send it to the local humane society, where there may be kitties who simply adore them.

How to Play With Your Cat

Playing with your cat may appear to be a no-brainer, but it simulates the hunting instinct in cats, so you need to be sure that you are doing it right. Although playtime can be lots of fun for both of you, there's a catch—you need to be sure that your cat is able to catch the "prey" once in a while and chew or scratch at it a bit. Otherwise, you will simply frustrate her, and she won't think the game is fun anymore. It's no fun to play a game if you never win, is it?

When you move the toy around on the pole or fishing line, do it in a way that resembles the natural movements of prey. Flop it around a bit like a wounded bird, or skitter it across the floor in erratic directions like a running mouse. My cat loves it when the prey "hides" behind something like a box or in between legs on a chair—anything that poses a challenge.

When you decide to stop playing, your cat may just walk away, but if she's still interested, you need to tone down the play. Allow your cat to catch the toy one more time before quitting. Substituting another toy she can play with on her own may help, especially if she's still raring to go.

Cat Trees and Cat Gyms

If you haven't invested in a cat tree or cat gym, complete with scratcher, you're missing out on doing your cat a favor. These are great for exercise, especially when combined with playtime.

Even if your cat hasn't shown much interest in the cat tree or gym, you can use it as a way to exercise her vertically while you are playing together. (Who says exercise can't be multidimensional?) She will love climbing to get at the toy you are teasing her with, and you'll be relieved that the cat tree you bought isn't a waste of money.

Boredom, frustration, and lack of exercise can cause cats to become aggressive. Diffuse pent-up energy by offering your feisty feline toys that stimulate her natural hunting instincts.

TIME AND PATIENCE

Although behavior problems such as aggression can be worrisome and frustrating, don't give up on your cat and decide that she's not worth the time or effort to make well again. Most cats turned into animal shelters have been given up on by their owners because they have problems such as this. Sadly, these cats are often considered "unadoptable" and are never given a second chance at having a good home. With a little patience, understanding, and reinforcement, you can have a more social, well-adjusted, and happy cat.

SO NOW YOU KNOW...

- The basic types of aggression are: play/prey aggression, sexual aggression, territorial aggression, overstimulation, redirected aggression, and fear/pain aggression.
- You can reduce aggression through interactive play and training.
- Spaying and neutering help reduce aggression by eliminating sexual tension.

CAT FURNITURE

Many cats become aggressive because they have too much pent-up energy. Like the teenager who has nothing to do, bored and frustrated cats start channeling their energy into things they shouldn't. Cat gyms are an excellent way to keep your cat out of trouble, entertained, and physically fit. Here are a number of places where you can purchase them:

CozyCatFurniture.com
Peshoni LLC
220 E. Delaware Avenue
Newark, DE 19711
Telephone and Fax: (302) 309-9183
E-mail: info@cozycatfurniture.com
Website: www.cozycatfurniture.com

Feline Furniture Company
P.O. Box 3379
Lake Arrowhead, CA 92352
Telephone: (909) 336-9414
Fax: (909) 336-9410
E-mail: FelineFurniture@gmail.com
Website: www.felinefurniture.com

House of Cats International
25011 Bell Mountain Drive
San Antonio, TX 78255
Telephone: (800) 889-7402
Fax: 210-698-3329
E-mail: houseofcats@aol.com
Website: www.houseofcatsintl.com

KatWALLks
Off The Wall Cat Furniture by Burdworks
P.O. Box 239
Wynona, Oklahoma 74084
Telephone:1-877-644-1615
E-mail: katwallks@earthlink.com
Website: www.katwallks.com

Playtime Workshop
406 Hawk St. STE D
Rockledge, FL 32955
Telephone: 321-631-9246
E-mail: customerservice@playtimeworkshop.com
Website: www.playtimeworkshop.com

Spoil My Kitty, LLC.
4278 New Irvine Rd.
Waco, KY 40385
Telephone: 888-403-2859
Website: www.spoilmykitty.com

Like the teenager who has nothing to do, bored and frustrated cats start channeling their energy into things they shouldn't. By playing with your cat several times a day, you give her an outlet for that energy and create a lasting bond with her as a result.

Types of Toys

When most people think of cat toys, they think about little fur mice or bags filled with catnip. The reality is that those are fine toys for your cat to play with on her own, but they aren't good to use when you play together. One reason for this is that you can accidentally get scratched when trying to grab the toy. More importantly, this can promote aggression because your cat will look at your hands as part of the toy. Ouch! The good news is that there are toys you can buy or make that allow you to safely interact with your cat.

Toys on long poles (commonly called teaser toys) and toys on fishing lines (called fishing toys) are excellent choices. These types of toys will keep your hands and feet safe from your kitty's claws while still providing hours of satisfying fun for your cat. You may be wondering about those battery-operated toys or toys that run on a track with which your kitty can play by herself. That isn't the point of the exercise here, and even if it were, some cats think that they're boring or scary. And even if your cat enjoys these toys, playing isn't just about wearing your cat down. It's also about bonding. By playing with your cat, you're building a positive bond with her.

It may take a bit of time and effort to determine which toys are best, but cat toys are fairly inexpensive, so you can experiment. Some fishing toys are actually set up so that you can easily replace the object at the end of the fishing pole (which also allows you to replaced a mangled toy). Some old standbys include feathers, Mylar ribbons, and fur or leather tassels, but the best toys are always the ones your cat likes. Just as with people, every cat has different tastes, so don't be afraid to try different things. If your cat finds a particular toy boring, send it to the local humane society, where there may be kitties who simply adore them.

How to Play With Your Cat

Playing with your cat may appear to be a no-brainer, but it simulates the hunting instinct in cats, so you need to be sure that you are doing it right. Although playtime can be lots of fun for both of you, there's a catch—you need to be sure that your cat is able to catch the "prey" once in a while and chew or scratch at it a bit. Otherwise, you will simply frustrate her, and she won't think the game is fun anymore. It's no fun to play a game if you never win, is it?

When you move the toy around on the pole or fishing line, do it in a way that resembles the natural movements of prey. Flop it around a bit like a wounded bird, or skitter it across the floor in erratic directions like a running mouse. My cat loves it when the prey "hides" behind something like a box or in between legs on a chair—anything that poses a challenge.

When you decide to stop playing, your cat may just walk away, but if she's still interested, you need to tone down the play. Allow your cat to catch the toy one more time before quitting. Substituting another toy she can play with on her own may help, especially if she's still raring to go.

Boredom, frustration, and lack of exercise can cause cats to become aggressive. Diffuse pent-up energy by offering your feisty feline toys that stimulate her natural hunting instincts.

Cat Trees and Cat Gyms

If you haven't invested in a cat tree or cat gym, complete with scratcher, you're missing out on doing your cat a favor. These are great for exercise, especially when combined with playtime.

Even if your cat hasn't shown much interest in the cat tree or gym, you can use it as a way to exercise her vertically while you are playing together. (Who says exercise can't be multidimensional?) She will love climbing to get at the toy you are teasing her with, and you'll be relieved that the cat tree you bought isn't a waste of money.

TIME AND PATIENCE

Although behavior problems such as aggression can be worrisome and frustrating, don't give up on your cat and decide that she's not worth the time or effort to make well again. Most cats turned into animal shelters have been given up on by their owners because they have problems such as this. Sadly, these cats are often considered "unadoptable" and are never given a second chance at having a good home. With a little patience, understanding, and reinforcement, you can have a more social, well-adjusted, and happy cat.

SO NOW YOU KNOW...

- The basic types of aggression are: play/prey aggression, sexual aggression, territorial aggression, overstimulation, redirected aggression, and fear/pain aggression.
- You can reduce aggression through interactive play and training.
- Spaying and neutering help reduce aggression by eliminating sexual tension.

CAT FURNITURE

Many cats become aggressive because they have too much pent-up energy. Like the teenager who has nothing to do, bored and frustrated cats start channeling their energy into things they shouldn't. Cat gyms are an excellent way to keep your cat out of trouble, entertained, and physically fit. Here are a number of places where you can purchase them:

CozyCatFurniture.com
Peshoni LLC
220 E. Delaware Avenue
Newark, DE 19711
Telephone and Fax: (302) 309-9183
E-mail: info@cozycatfurniture.com
Website: www.cozycatfurniture.com

Feline Furniture Company
P.O. Box 3379
Lake Arrowhead, CA 92352
Telephone: (909) 336-9414
Fax: (909) 336-9410
E-mail: FelineFurniture@gmail.com
Website: www.felinefurniture.com

House of Cats International
25011 Bell Mountain Drive
San Antonio, TX 78255
Telephone: (800) 889-7402
Fax: 210-698-3329
E-mail: houseofcats@aol.com
Website: www.houseofcatsintl.com

KatWALLks
Off The Wall Cat Furniture by Burdworks
P.O. Box 239
Wynona, Oklahoma 74084
Telephone:1-877-644-1615
E-mail: katwallks@earthlink.com
Website: www.katwallks.com

Playtime Workshop
406 Hawk St. STE D
Rockledge, FL 32955
Telephone: 321-631-9246
E-mail: customerservice@playtimeworkshop.com
Website: www.playtimeworkshop.com

Spoil My Kitty, LLC.
4278 New Irvine Rd.
Waco, KY 40385
Telephone: 888-403-2859
Website: www.spoilmykitty.com

Cats come practically housetrained, which is a godsend. You don't have to do much more than show a cat her litter box, and when the need arises, she's there answering the call of nature. But oddly enough, the number-one reason owners cite when giving up their felines is urination outside of the litter box.

Chapter 7

Thinking Outside the Box: Litter Box Woes

You don't have to housetrain a kitten. Kittens instinctively know how to use the litter box, and therefore it's unlikely you'll have to clean up many accidents. However, be sure that the litter box is in an accessible place and that the walls of the box aren't so tall that your tiny kitten can't climb into it. Also, be sure that your kitten knows where it is. You can do this by putting her in the box several times. Once she can find it on her own— and she may need a reminder because kittens can be forgetful—she'll use the litter box the rest of her life. Unless, of course, there's a problem.

Believe it or not, your kitty prefers to use her litter box. Cats don't want to eliminate where they eat, sleep, or hang out; they're preprogrammed to be fastidious in this area. If your kitty is urinating outside the box or doesn't seem to be using it, something is dreadfully wrong. Unfortunately, your kitty can't verbalize what the problem is. It's up to you to figure it out—and soon—or she's going to get used to not using her toilet area at all.

GETTING BACK INTO THE BOX

When your cat stops using her litter box, it's time for a serious assessment of what is really going on. Some kittens just don't get the hang of it, and older cats may develop the bad habit of eliminating in inappropriate places for emotional or medical reasons. Whatever the issue, it may be important for your cat's health and your sanity to get the problem figured out as soon as possible. So let's look at some possible reasons for this behavior.

LITTER BOX ABANDONMENT

Have you ever gone into a bathroom at a gas station and it was totally icky? The whole place smelled awful and the stall wasn't very clean. You had to hold your breath the entire time, and then you discovered that the toilet wouldn't flush. Not a pleasant experience, was it? If you're particular, you may have even waited, with legs crossed, until you got to the next gas station, hoping it would be a more welcoming place.

Now, think about how your cat may feel about her litter box. Is it sparkling clean, or is it smelly and icky? Does she have to avoid kitty land mines, or does she have a clean place to walk? What may smell okay to you isn't necessarily pleasant to her. If she doesn't like the cleaning agent you're using or the way the litter box is cleaned, she may be expressing her displeasure over this. Remember, your cat can't just tell you it's time to clean the litter box, but she *will* avoid it if it is really unpleasant. After all, she can't cross her legs and wait until the next litter box pops up along the side of the road.

Keep It Clean

If you suspect that a dirty "bathroom" is the source of your cat's litter box problem, the easiest thing to do is clean it more often. That means frequently dumping the old litter and replacing it with fresh litter on a regular, perhaps scheduled basis, along with removing feces every day with a cat poop scoop. Every day, you ask? Yes, every day.

Use the following guidelines for changing litter:

- standard clay litters: once a week
- recycled newspaper litters: once a week
- scoopable litters: at least once a month
- natural scoopable litters: at least once a month
- crystal (silicon) litters: at least once a month

How often you change the litter depends largely on the material it's made from and its ability to absorb waste. If soiled litter materials are properly collected each day, you will be able to get rid of both the urine and the feces effectively, thus leaving the litter box looking and smelling cleaner longer.

Kittens can train themselves to use the litter box almost immediately. If your cat is urinating outside the box or doesn't seem to be using it, something is dreadfully wrong.

Because cats have such a strong sense of smell, some may be positively picky when it comes to their litter boxes. The smell of perfumes or added scents, like those used in litter fresheners, will probably make their toilet area highly offensive to them (even though it smells just fine to us). If your cat is avoiding the litter box, change the litter or find one that is unscented.

The problem many people have with scooping and cleaning the litter box is, well, scooping and cleaning the litter box. It's a dirty job, but someone has to do it! But wait, don't self-cleaning litter boxes exist? Yes, they do. It's debatable how effective they really are at cleaning up the waste (you must use clumping litter with these) and whether they're traumatizing to a cat. Basically, they work by using sensors and a timing device. A self-cleaning box detects that your cat has gone into it and waits a certain amount of time (between five and ten minutes) before triggering a mechanism that begins the cycle to scoop out the clumped, used litter. Depending on your cat and her habits (or whether you have several cats), these litter boxes may do their cleaning while your cat is still nearby. If you have a feline who is easily spooked, the ruckus may be enough incentive to keep her away.

No litter box relieves you of the need to change the litter and do a thorough cleaning on a regular basis. Still, self-cleaners keep the scooping down to a bare minimum, which may make a big difference for those people who simply can't bear to scoop.

Here are a few websites on which you can research some options:

- The Litter-Robot: www.litter-robot.com
- Littermaid Litter Box: www.littermaid.com
- Omega Paw Self Cleaning Litter Box: www.radiofence.com
- Purrforma Plus Litter Box: www.petmate.com

Keeping your cat's litter box clean is the first step toward determining why she is urinating inappropriately. Remember that her nose is far more sensitive than yours, so even if the box smells okay to you, it may not smell good to her. Maintaining a clean litter box should be your number-one priority after feeding your cat and making sure that she has clean, fresh water daily. I guarantee that your cat will appreciate your effort.

Try a New Location

Location, location, location. Oddly enough, your cat can stop using the litter box because she doesn't like where you've put it. If she can't get to it because it is in some hard-to-reach, out-of-the way corner, or if she is upstairs and her litter box is downstairs, she may not think about (or feel like) running downstairs to use it. That's why you should have at least one litter box on every level of the house. Likewise, for every cat there should be one litter box. Why is that? Well, not every cat is willing to share. However, you don't need a litter box for each cat on every level of the house.

Location in the room is important, too. Some cats like their privacy. Other cats like to be able to see from their vantage point. It's a matter of taste. In most cases, selecting a place that doesn't get a lot of traffic is best, provided your cat has completely free and easy access to it.

Problems can also occur because you've decided to move the litter box. Your cat may decide that the location rather than the type of box used is important. In this case, you may have a tough time moving your cat's litter box and will have to return it to its original spot.

Try a Different Shape or Size

The next step in determining why your cat is urinating outside the box is to look at the box itself. Not all boxes fit all cats. If you have a large cat who is feeling

Because they are extremely clean animals, cats may abandon their litter box if it's dirty. Proper litter box maintenance is crucial to your feline companion's care.

a bit claustrophobic in a covered litter box, you may have to change to a bigger box that is either open or big enough not to disturb her. Some boxes, even when open, are just too small. If you have a large cat, you may have to make your own box if you can't buy one that offers a comfortable fit. Some plastic storage containers may work if you cut them down enough so that your cat can easily walk into them.

On the flip side of this issue is that the litter box may be too big for your cat. Kittens and some smaller cats may have a tough time with high-walled litter boxes. If this is the case, try cutting down the box's sides or use a jelly roll pan (a cookie sheet with high sides) or any other low-walled pan, especially for youngsters and seniors.

Try a Different Type of Litter

Litter type seems like an odd reason for a cat not to use her litter box, but there are valid reasons for this. And regardless of what you would prefer to use, most finicky felines have their individual preferences.

Many cats find that standard clay litter is the wrong texture and that it's sharp on their paws. Often, the litter is scented with perfumes, which irritates their nose. Most cats prefer softer litter, such as clumping litter or even litter made from natural ingredients such as wheat or corn. Sometimes the type of litter your cat was raised with makes a difference because she may not recognize a new type as something in which to eliminate. In other words, if you change her litter, she may get confused.

Once you find a brand your cat likes, stick with it. Cats don't like variety in most things, especially in this area. And obviously, you're probably not going to get away with using whatever is on sale.

One more thing: Some owners like to use litter box liners to make cleanup easier. However, your cat may not like that idea either, so skip the liners. If you really object to cleaning out the box and replacing the litter, you can buy inexpensive, disposable litter trays. There are even disposable cat litter boxes with the litter already in them! They are not particularly environmentally friendly but provide an alternative if you just can't handle cleaning the litter box.

INAPPROPRIATE ELIMINATION

Health problems can invariably cause a cat to "think outside the box." This is a biggie because, quite frankly, a cat who doesn't feel good is more likely not to make it to her litter box all the time or to blame her litter box for her condition.

Cat logic is pretty simple when it comes to pain: Avoid whatever is causing it. Your cat isn't thinking "My body is causing me pain" but rather "Something in my environment is causing me pain." If she has a urinary tract infection, extreme constipation, arthritis, or anything that causes her to hurt while eliminating, she's going to think that where she's doing it (namely, the litter box) is causing the problem. Because she needs to eliminate, she'll try *different* places to see if things go any better. Or maybe a particular place seems to be less painful for her—you never know.

If you are sure that your cat isn't urinating outside the box in protest of a stinky toilet area, the next step is to determine if there is anything physically or emotionally wrong with her.

If your cat is house soiling, she may have an aversion to the type of litter box or litter you are using.

Get a Health Check

A number of ailments and conditions can cause your cat pain during or after elimination. These include urinary tract infections, extreme constipation, irritable bowel syndrome, megacolon, some forms of cancer, and senility, among others. Your next step, then, must be to take your kitty to the veterinarian for a thorough examination. He may want to run several tests to rule out each possibility. Once he has determined the source of the problem, he will most likely prescribe medication. Follow your veterinarian's advice to the letter. If the problem hasn't been going on for too long, your kitty will most likely start using her box again once she feels better. If she doesn't, you may have to retrain her to use it again.

Retraining Kitty to Use the Litter Box

Once your cat develops an aversion to her litter

box, it may be very difficult for her to think about using it again. After all, she's now perfectly happy eliminating elsewhere.

The first step in the retraining process is to clean up any areas your kitty has been using as a bathroom with a good enzymatic cleaner, which will remove every last trace of the smell. As long as your cat can locate the odor in those locations, she will continue to make them her toilet. You can also use a boundary-type spray on these areas, although you may have to use it daily to discourage future accidents. Double-sided sticky tape is another option; it will keep your cat from wanting to touch those areas because it feels unpleasant on her sensitive paws. If your cat is spraying the area, use some kitty pheromones after cleaning it.

Next, provide a *clean* litter box of the *right size* and containing the *correct* type of litter. It's often a good idea to place the box near the offending area.

INAPPROPRIATE MARKING/SPRAYING

You've cleaned the litter box and had your veterinarian examine your kitty, and she's healthy. And yet she's spraying along the wall. What's going on?

Most likely, your kitty is marking, not urinating, per se (although it's the same stuff!). However, marking has to do with insecurity issues and the presence of unfamiliar things.

For years, I was under the impression that only male cats marked, but that's untrue. Both males and females mark their territory. Marking consists of spraying urine, often on a vertical surface. It's your cat's way of announcing her presence—a "calling card," so to speak. Cats who mark often are usually intact, but spayed and neutered cats can also mark at any time.

Marking often occurs when there is tension among cats. Outdoor cats who roam around near your home can even cause an indoor cat to mark. While you may not know about those strays, your cat certainly does. You're likely to see marking when you introduce a new pet, new surroundings, or maybe even an unfamiliar human visitor or home service person.

Reestablish Security in the Environment

Cats typically mark when there are stressors or changes in their environment. When a cat marks, it means "Hey, this is my turf!" to any interloper that might be hanging around. The best way to deal with the problem generally rests in trying to diffuse whatever stress is causing the need for your cat to keep reasserting herself.

Unfortunately, you can't simply tell your cat to calm down and deal with the situation. Because she has spectacular senses, your cat can hear, see, and sometimes even smell the offending intruders, even when you can't. This makes her insecure

Litter Box Requirements

Cats are fastidious creatures. They don't want to eliminate where they eat or sleep. If your cat stops using her litter box, she has a good reason for doing so. Some kittens just don't get the hang of it, and older cats may develop the bad habit of eliminating in inappropriate places for emotional or medical reasons. When selecting a litter box for your cat, consider the following:

- Are the sides of the litter box too high or too low? Small cats or seniors may find it difficult to climb into a litter box with high sides, and low sides allow a cat to hang outside the litter box, which may make her feel insecure.

- Is the box too big? Cats can sometimes feel lost or vulnerable in a litter box that is too big for them.

- Is the automatic mechanism in your self-cleaning box very loud? Some cats are frightened by the noise these boxes make and will refuse to use them.

- Is the litter inside the litter box too deep or too shallow? If it's too deep, your cat will feel uncomfortable putting her paws into it. If it's too shallow, it's not fun to dig in and doesn't offer sufficient coverage. One inch (2.5 cm) is comfortable for most cats.

- Is the box in a convenient and not too crowded location? Cats need to get to their litter boxes easily, and they often want privacy when using their bathrooms.

and prompts her to keep marking her indoor turf to make certain that they know the place or thing is off-limits. Fortunately, there are ways to make her feel more comfortable and happier with the status quo. One way is to use special cat pheromones. They have a similar smell to the natural pheromones cats release from their cheeks when they rub them against the objects they want to claim as their own, much like a smell ID. (These are available through www.feliway.com.) By using both the diffuser and the spray scents, you can signal to your cat that this is indeed her territory and everything is okay.

As a general rule, each cat in your household should have her own litter box.

If your cat is worried about outside intruders, keeping the shutters closed and the curtains drawn is a good idea. (Essentially, what she can't see can't hurt her state of mind.) You can also buy cat repellant and use it consistently in your yard, where stray cats tend to roam. Many brands are available at pet-supply stores, on the Internet, and through catalog stores. Follow the directions on the label, and be sure that the brand you use is nontoxic.

If your cat is intact, neutering will reduce the urge to spray as well.

OTHER CAUSES

There may be other reasons why your cat isn't using her litter box, but the ones described in this chapter are the most common. Other potential causes may have more to do with your cat having a negative experience associated with a particular litter box or a particular location. For example, if your cat likes doing her business in the garage litter box but the family dog has come by to pester her more than a few times, she's unlikely to use the litter box in that location very often. If he's allowed to continue bothering her or causes her to run when he sees her in the area, she won't come back at all. Guess what will happen if you don't have another litter box set up in the house?

Other reasons for litter box problems may be precipitated by fear behavior, such as getting pounced on by other cats, loud noises, crowded areas, or any number of environmental stressors. Then, there may be a cause you just can't figure out.

Basically, you need to make your cat's litter box as attractive as possible and make the areas where she is inappropriately relieving herself as unattractive as possible. Your cat's instincts will do the rest. If you still have problems, consult your veterinarian or a pet behaviorist.

SO NOW YOU KNOW...

- Some inappropriate elimination problems have to do with a cat not wanting to use a dirty litter box. The best thing you can do is keep the litter box as clean as possible at all times.
- Self-cleaning litter boxes can be useful for people who don't want to scoop regularly, but they aren't a substitute for cleaning the litter box or replacing the litter.
- The size, shape, and location of the litter box may affect whether your cat uses it.
- Cats have preferences for litter, so choose the one your cat likes and stick with it.
- Litter box problems could stem from a biological source, and cats who have health problems avoid using them because they think that the litter box is the cause of their pain.
- Other litter box problems can be precipitated by fear behavior, such as intimidation by other pets, loud noises, crowded areas, or any number of environmental stressors.

You love your cat, but you hate that she shreds your furniture and mangles other assorted personal items. You've bought her scratching posts, but she isn't interested. You're at wit's end and just about ready to make that dreaded appointment to get her declawed.

Chapter 8

Staying in Shape: Scratching

But before you do, consider the fact that you really can discourage her from scratching inappropriately by simply being smarter about the means and methods you use to keep her from doing so. Believe it or not, there are solutions that will satisfy both of you.

WHY CATS SCRATCH

As mentioned in Chapter 1, cats scratch for a variety of reasons. They scratch to sharpen their claws, to mark their territory, to reduce stress, and to exercise. Scratching is a completely normal feline behavior. Whether wild or domestic, you can't stop a cat from doing it. It's instinctive—so much so that even declawed cats will keep trying to do it! If you don't want a feline companion who scratches, buy a stuffed toy in the shape of a cat.

Scratch That!

You wouldn't mind so much if all that your cat ever scratched was her scratching post. But instead, all she wants to paw at is the new furniture. What's a frustrated pet parent to do?

All cats are compelled to scratch as part of their natural behavior. They scratch to sharpen their claws, to mark their territory, to reduce stress, and to exercise.

First, step back and consider the situation. Your cat isn't being naughty. She merely wants a satisfying place to scratch, and she doesn't recognize that you paid an arm and a leg for that couch. All she knows is that it feels good to scratch there and that it's just the right surface and texture she's looking for.

Cats *need* to scratch, plain and simple. They mark territory by sharpening their claws on various surfaces because doing so leaves behind both a visual marker and a scent marker from the glands on their feet. But aside from marking and feeling good, scratching is also used as a grooming aid. Scratching on a post helps remove the dead parts of the nail, thus making it thinner and sharper. Nails that have not been trimmed for a long time may grow in a circular shape, causing the tips to grow into the cat's paw pad, or they may become too thick, which sometimes happens with older or less active cats. This can be extremely painful for them, and it can also lead to infection. So you see, cats take full advantage of these all-purpose claws, and they're not going to be convinced that they should behave otherwise.

Nevertheless, the trick to stopping your kitty from claiming your couch as a huge kitty "nail file" and directing her toward a better place to scratch is actually quite simple: You must make the areas she's scratching unappealing to her and the scratchers you give her hard to resist.

But what about declawing or tendonectomies, you ask? So many veterinarians still perform these procedures that you might feel tempted to skip all the extra trouble and training and go for the shortcut. After all, if vets think it's okay, it can't be that bad, right? Wrong. As I've already explained, declawing is a terribly painful lifelong experience for any cat. There are safer, more humane, and more effective alternatives to declawing. You really don't have to go to the extreme of removing your cat's digits just to save your furniture. Depending on your needs, you can still opt for a quick fix, but a long-term solution is always best if you want to reestablish household harmony and keep everybody happy.

Tendonectomy

Tendonectomy, that is, severing the tendons, involves cutting the flexor tendons on the underside of your cats fingers. Look at your own fingers and imagine what it would be like if you couldn't open or close your hand. How vulnerable would you feel if your fingers flopped around and you couldn't tighten or flex them? With these tendons severed your cat can't scratch properly. This surgery isn't appropriate or fair to your cat.

QUICK FIXES

There are fairly simple ways to reduce scratching on inappropriate items. Let's look at some of the easier solutions first.

Clipping

Oddly enough, one of the easiest things you can do to reduce scratching simply has to do with basic care. Trimming your cat's nails once a week to keep them short goes a long way toward curbing her urge to claw. It won't eliminate the need, though, so you'll still have to implement other methods to keep her from scratching the wrong items.

Clipping your cat's claws is generally easy if she has white or clear nails. Dark nails make the chore more difficult because you can't see the quick, which is the pink part of the nail where the blood vessels and nerves are located. If you cut into the quick (called "quicking"), your cat will bleed and experience pain, and she is unlikely to let you clip her nails again.

When you trim your cat's nails, use cutters made specifically for cat's claws. Trim only that section where the nail narrows. (Don't cut the thick part of the nail.) If you can see the quick (the pink part of the nail), clip the white part of the nail

Trimming your cat's nails once a week to keep them short goes a long way toward curbing her urge to claw.

just below it. If you do this every week, the quick will shorten and the entire claw will become naturally short as a result.

Getting your cat used to nail cutting might be a bit of a struggle at first, so go slowly. Many felines don't like to be held long, nor do they like to have their feet held. When grooming a scaredy cat, start by gently holding her in your lap and gently touching or holding her paws for a second or two. If she struggles or becomes frantic, let her go and try again when she is more relaxed and willing to accept being touched. It will take some time, but once she allows you to touch all her feet, you can begin clipping her nails. Do it slowly and carefully. If it becomes a struggle, try doing it when she's sleepy and less likely to fight.

If you need help or don't feel comfortable trimming the nails yourself, have your veterinarian or a professional cat-friendly groomer clip your cat's claws or show you how to do it properly.

Nail Caps

When considering product assistance, nail caps (such as Soft Paws) are the quickest and least painful way to put an end to inappropriate scratching right away. These are soft rubber caps that fit over your cat's nails. Either you or your veterinarian can apply them. They are put on individually with a special type of glue, but it's necessary to trim your cat's nails before doing so. They come in natural or various other colors for a flashier look.

Nail caps aren't a cure-all. They don't stop the scratching instinct, and eventually your cat's nails will grow out, causing the caps to fall off. But they're an effective and painless stopgap until you can implement other long-term changes, like retraining your feisty feline.

Sticky Tape

There are many brands of sticky tape available, but I mention Sticky Paws by name because it's simply the most effective and safest product of its kind out there to deter cats from clawing. Packaged in strips, all you need to do is peel off the backing and adhere it to all the objects your cat loves to scratch. (Sticky Paws warns against using the strips on leather furniture, but it's been my experience that you can clean off adhesive residue with a good leather cleaner if any is left behind after removal.)

This is a great product, and it couldn't be easier to use. Cats hate putting

DID YOU KNOW?

You may be wondering if standard double-sided tape will work in a pinch over Sticky Paws. The answer is a qualified maybe. Sticky Paws has been developed and tested to ensure pet safety, and it also doesn't leave tape marks on furniture when used correctly. While other double-sided tape will do the job well enough, you'll want the guarantee of a product that has been tested with cats.

their paws on anything sticky, and when they touch Sticky Paws, they will almost immediately decide that it's an uncomfortable surface that's not at all appealing. This is such an effective deterrent that most cats will even make an extra effort to seek out something more desirable—which includes that scratcher you put right beside it, right? Sticky Paws also makes long cardboard scratchers that lay on the floor, which come in handy if your cat has taken a liking to your carpeting or hardwood floors.

The downside to the sticky tape method is that the strips have a tendency to gather dirt and hair. This means that you must check and replace them regularly lest the tape lose its stickiness—and lest your cat decide that it's not creepy after all and start scratching your things again.

Boundary Sprays

There are several versions of boundary sprays on the market. Once again, it doesn't get easier than this: Just spray them once a day on places you don't want your cat to go. These sprays work because they incorporate a scent cats simply detest. A few sniffs and your kitty will hightail it in the opposite direction.

Boundary sprays are very effective, but they have some drawbacks. First, you might find that they smell strange to you. Spraying the sofa or furnishing in question is fine, but the smell might be enough of a repellant to keep your cat *far away* from the sofa—and the scratcher. The boundary sprays don't work longer than 24 hours, so you have to remember to refresh them or your cat will be back at it again.

Static Mats and Other Deterrents

Depending on your cat's particular taste for scratching, you may be able to keep her off certain pieces of furniture and away from other tempting objects or areas in your home by using a static mat or a similar electronic type of device. Basically, a static mat is a thin vinyl mat that has wiring run through it. Hooked to a battery, it emits a small electrical charge when it's stepped on but one that is no more powerful or painful than the static charge you get running along the carpet in your stocking feet. With pets, it's beneficial for its "shock value." Static mats are good for flat, horizontal surfaces.

There's another electronic deterrent called SSSCAT that works by using a motion sensor connected to a canister of air. When the cat approaches the forbidden place, it emits a startling tone and then follows it up with a blast of hissing air. Cats really hate the air blast and associate the tone with this blast. Eventually, just the sound of the tone will send your kitty running.

Other versions of repellants include passive mats with nubs on them. The idea behind these is that your cat won't like their uncomfortable texture and will leave the area alone. Laying down aluminum foil also works because many cats detest the odd feel of it and the crinkly sound it makes.

Some of these methods may not necessarily work as well as others specifically as a scratching deterrent because the area being scratched is often vertical. Also, static mats and other boundary devices may fail if you're simply trying to keep your cat away from an object—cats can jump over them. And then there's obviously a problem if you want to use the furniture you are trying to protect from your cat. I don't recommend sitting on a static mat, and while using fake mats might work, you wouldn't want to restrict your own access to the furniture. But then you may be all right with having your kitty sleep on the sofa, you just don't want her scratching it. SSSCAT may be your best option as a quick fix because it doesn't matter if the area is vertical or horizontal. It may be a little indiscriminant, though, when it comes to who is being trained—it may hiss at you as you walk by!

Feline Pheromones

If you don't mind sharing but can't abide the destructive aspect of scratching,

Spraying feline pheromones can help keep your cat's scratching under control because the calming scent works to reduce her need to mark her territory.

pheromones are another potential way to keep things under control, especially if your cat is feeling particularly stressed. Feliway makes both a spray and an automatic atomizer that produce calming scents, and they are easy to apply in a variety of circumstances. Although pheromones help calm your cat by reducing her need to mark her territory, they won't completely stop her from scratching inappropriate items, so always use the pheromones in conjunction with training.

LONG-TERM FIXES

Although quick fixes are tempting, it's fairer to your cat to retrain her in the art of appropriate indoor scratching. The end result is a more harmonious environment for all concerned—and better-looking furniture!

Training to Redirect Scratching

Training your cat to scratch more appropriate items (namely scratchers and cat furniture) might seem monumental at first, but it's really not. When cats figure out the right things to scratch, most will go at them with wanton abandon, especially if the scratchers you choose suit your feline's particular preferences.

If your cat is scratching something inappropriate, like your brand-new sofa, she has already determined where she needs to have her scratchers. Placing a scratching post or cat tree near all her favorite scratching objects isn't a bad idea. In fact, your cat may simply go to them and leave your furniture alone once she sees how much more fun they can be.

Discouraging scratching on inappropriate objects by making them unavailable or unpleasant will usually be enough to make your cat look for something else on which to leave her mark. But having a variety of appropriate options that require minimal effort because they are within easy access will often solve most scratching problems as well. And if the scratcher really feels good, the decision will be a no-brainer for her.

Choosing Scratchers

Believe it or not, choosing the right scratcher is just as important as having a scratcher in the first place. A scratcher won't do your cat (or your furniture) a

Scratching Preferences

Cats have different scratching preferences. Some love to sprawl out lengthwise and have a really good stretch along with a scratch. Others love vertical scratchers that they can really sink their claws into. Look closely at what your cat is currently scratching in the house and find a scratcher that satisfies that need: vertical or horizontal; plush carpet, rough wood, or sisal; etc.

bit of good if it's the wrong type because she just won't use it. Your cat needs an alternative that makes her feel good.

Types of Scratchers

There is a variety of scratchers available on the market, but they basically come in two types: vertical and horizontal. Occasionally, you'll find scratchers that are set on an angle, and most cats love those, too. The horizontal ones are usually inexpensive and made from cardboard, although they can be made from other materials. Vertical scratchers come in a number of types and styles, some basic and some quite fancy. When shopping for one, keep the following in mind:

- If you are looking for a vertical scratcher, choose one with a wide, sturdy base. Your cat needs to feel that it is a safe and stable place to scratch against.
- Scratchers can be made of cardboard, wood, carpet, or sisal. You should try all types to see what your cat prefers. The important thing is that she can really sink her claws into it.
- Vertical and horizontal scratchers should be long enough that your cat can

Placing a scratching post or cat tree near all your feline's favorite scratching objects is a good way to redirect scratching away from inappropriate items such as your sofa.

get a good stretch as well as a good scratch.

- Don't limit your cat to just one kind of scratcher. Give her plenty of opportunities to scratch different materials in various designs so that she can decide which works best; this will hopefully stem her inclination to experiment elsewhere.
- Try to provide at least one scratcher that's combined with a cat tree or kitty house so that your cat can climb and perch.

Scratcher Locations

Location and easy access are just as important as having scratchers your cat likes. She will use a scratcher more often than your furniture if it is convenient for her to do so. Scratchers should be strategically placed where your cat will naturally spend most of her time. These locations include:

- anywhere you and your family spend time
- near the furnishings your cat likes to scratch
- near the front door
- near her bed and napping places

If you need to convince your cat that the scratcher is indeed more interesting than your own furnishings, try sprinkling catnip on it. If your cat enjoys catnip, it will make it a more enticing option. If she doesn't react to catnip, try attaching a favorite toy to it or playing around it with a teaser toy. Once she paws at it, she may just think that it's the cat's meow.

Choosing Cat Trees

Cat trees are important items for indoor cats because they provide necessary mental stimulation and exercise. While they may not match your decor exactly

Make Your Own Scratcher

You can make a very inexpensive scratcher by affixing upside-down carpeting (the rough side) on a piece of wood. Or you can also use swatches of inexpensive industrial carpet right side up on the wood. A pine log with bark on it placed flat on the ground also works well. Of course, if you are really handy, you might try your hand at a vertical scratching post. You can get everything you need at a local home and hardware store.

(and by the way, there are manufacturers that will make them to order!), they will certainly save your decor. Besides, cats love climbing and hiding in cubbyholes, so a cat tree is an absolute must for any happy kitty household.

The rule of thumb with these items is the bigger and more elaborate, the better. But if you're on a budget, consider at least buying or making one that includes a platform that your kitty can climb up to and on which she can perch. Trees with multiple platforms and hidey-holes are always better, but your cat can still enjoy a simple tree that provides a place on which to nap and scratch. Most trees are carpeted and have sisal and cardboard incorporated as scratching surfaces. And if the cat tree you already have doesn't include a scratcher, you can always position one next to it.

The main thing to keep in mind when selecting a cat tree is that it *must* be sturdy and it *must not* look flimsy. If it feels unsteady or even looks unreliable, your finicky feline won't use it and you'll have gone through all that trouble and expense for nothing. As with scratchers, the best way to get your cat to use the cat tree is to sprinkle catnip on it and play with a teaser toy around it. She'll soon be enjoying the tree in no time.

The more available and convenient you make appropriate scratching areas, the less likely your cat will be to use inappropriate ones.

SO NOW YOU KNOW...

- Cats need to scratch. Even cats who have been declawed still have the instinct to scratch.
- You can temporarily eliminate scratching by using nail caps.
- You can reduce the urge to scratch by trimming your cat's claws regularly.
- You can keep your cat from scratching furniture and other items with the use of sticky tapes, boundary sprays, static mats, pheromones, and other tools.
- You can teach your cat to use scratchers by making them more appealing than the inappropriate items she's been scratching and by placing them strategically near things she likes to scratch.
- You should have plenty of cat scratchers and trees available for your cat throughout your home.

Lately you've been noticing that your houseplants have been trashed. Perhaps you've found dirt scattered across the floor or your plants ripped to shreds. Or maybe you found your garden dug up. Then one day, you discovered the culprit in the act—it was your cat!

Chapter 9

Marking Territory: Digging and Chewing

You've tried everything you know to keep your rambunctious kitty away from your plants, but nothing has seemed to work. You're at your wit's end.

Keeping your greenery intact as well as keeping your cat from ingesting the poisonous substances found in some houseplants can be a challenge, but training and a bit of rearranging can help redirect your cat's focus toward better choices.

WHY YOUR CAT LIKES TO DIG

Plants are vertical, and they often have a pleasing smell that entices cats. The dirt they are in is soft and pleasant to their feet and claws, and once a cat has made her mark in it, it smells like her, especially if she has urinated or defecated in it. You may notice that when your cat enters her litter box, she will first sniff the litter, then dig for a short time, squat near the area of digging, turn to smell her waste, and then dig once again.

Digging and covering waste are probably rooted in the wild cat's tendency to hide urine and feces; doing so helps cover her trail and may keep her healthier by reducing parasite transmission. In some cases, cats mark their territory with urine or feces and will leave the deposits uncovered to assert their presence to other cats.

In the wild, cats dig and cover their waste to hide their presence from predators. Likewise, they will mark their territory with uncovered waste to assert their dominance to other cats.

All this goes to show that tearing up plants and digging in the dirt are behaviors that are completely natural to your cat. Even if the plants in your home are your prized possessions, it makes no difference to her. She simply wants to make her mark in the world, and those plants are an enticing place to do it—especially if you haven't given her any other alternatives.

WHY YOUR CAT CHEWS YOUR PLANTS

Besides marking their territory, cats chew on plants because they may need extra roughage or greenery in their diets. If you must keep indoor plants despite the ongoing chore of keeping your kitty's paws off them, the first thing you need to do is make sure that they aren't toxic to her. Common dangerous varieties include lilies, sago palms, azaleas, rhododendrons, and tulips.

The next step is to keep plants on which your kitty will enjoy nibbling. Special greens such as wheatgrass and catnip can be turned into a windowsill garden that she is allowed to visit whenever the fancy strikes her. Many pet-supply stores sell them, or in the case of catnip, you can buy seeds and grow them from scratch (so to speak). You can also put the acceptable plants in a place where your kitty likes to sunbathe or in another area where she enjoys relaxing.

PET-PROOFING YOUR PLANTS

Now that you have protected your cat from your plants, you need to protect your plants from your cat.

First, redirect her attention elsewhere by giving her the opportunity to engage in a different activity that she may find satisfying. For example, if your cat is scratching the plants in an effort to mark them,

Dangerous Plants

Having plants in your home can be hazardous to your kitty's health because many of the ones commonly kept can be poisonous if ingested. If you must have greenery, select a variety that is nontoxic. The ASPCA provides a listing of both safe and unsafe plants on their website at www.aspca.org. Click on the site's animal poison control center page and select the appropriate link. Also keep in mind that while you can prevent your cat from getting into dangerous plants in your home, it's more difficult to protect her if she goes outdoors, especially if she's allowed to roam unsupervised.

If you think that your cat has ingested something toxic, you can reach the ASPCA Animal Poison Control Center hotline at (888) 426-4435. This center is open 24 hours a day, 7 days a week, 365 days a year, and it is staffed with the best experts in animal poison control. A consultation fee may be charged to your credit card, but this is on a per-incident basis (not a per-call basis), and you can call as many times as you need to obtain advice about your particular crisis.

try putting a scratcher near them. If this doesn't work, you can protect your plants in several other ways:

- Hang your plants on a hook out of the jumping and climbing reach of your cat.
- Spray the leaves of your plants with a mild solution of soap and water or cat repellant.
- Use a product such as Sticky Paws made specifically for plants. The sticky strips go in a crisscross shape over the top of the soil in the planter, making the plants less inviting for digging.
- Use a product such as SSSCAT. The loud noise it makes will discourage your cat every time she approaches the plants and may keep her away from the area entirely.
- Surround the plants with static shock mats. The mild shock will deter your cat from stepping near them.
- If your cat has been using the planters as a litter box, consider switching to a softer litter in her litter box if she is using hard clay. Switch to a biodegradable wheat or corn litter that feels more like soil or a softer clumping clay. (Feel it with your hands to be sure that it is the right texture.)
- Provide a substitute for whatever your cat is seeking (texture, roughage, etc.) when she resorts to wreaking havoc on your plants by looking for the qualities that most mimic the one she repeatedly visits. For example, wood, sisal, or dried grasses might do the trick.
- If all else fails, move your plants to a location that is off-limits to your cat, such as a room that can be closed off from the rest of the house.

Cats chew on plants because they may need extra roughage in their diets to aid digestion. Be sure that the plants that you keep are not toxic to your cat.

Remember that you'll have to keep the mats, SSSCAT, and other items in place for several weeks to several months until your cat has forgotten her old behaviors and learned the new ones, namely leaving your plants alone and only dining on the cat-edible plants in her kitty garden. You might also consider making the extra scratchers, special greens, and new litter permanent fixtures in your home.

By giving your cat something that will satisfy

Edible Cat Gardens

To keep your cat from chewing on and digging up your houseplants, provide her with her very own garden. This is particularly important for cats who can't chew on grass outdoors. Cats normally crave roughage to aid them in their digestion and will eat grass when they have access to it, but it may not always be safe for them to eat because it may be sprayed with pesticides. You can provide your indoor cat with cat greens and freshly grown catnip, all of which are easy to grow and can be bought at most pet stores or garden centers.

her urgings and by limiting or removing access to the plants you don't want her getting into, you both will enjoy the continued pleasure of having that beautiful greenery in your home.

SO NOW YOU KNOW...

- Cats love to dig in soil because it feels good to their paws.
- Cats scratch and tear up plants to mark their territory.
- Many common houseplants are poisonous to cats; the ASPCA provides a listing of toxic varieties on its website.
- Provide healthy and safe plants for your cat to chew on, like wheatgrass and catnip.
- You can keep your cats away from your plants by using a variety of simple deterrents.

You can help keep your cat from digging and chewing by providing healthy, safe plants for her to chew on, like wheatgrass and catnip.

It all starts quite innocuously. You notice holes in a few of your socks. Then you notice that a blanket is wet or that it has a few holes in it, too. Then something else more important gets ruined, like your favorite sweater. Or maybe the laundry you just washed and dried still feels wet in spots. Eventually, you discover that your cat has been chewing and sucking on your clothing (especially wool), but you don't know why.

Chapter 10

Feeling Needy: Wool Sucking

You're tired of having to redo the laundry and not very pleased about having to replace your ruined clothes. What do you do? Although it's usually a harmless habit (well, for your cat), it can be difficult to cope with having your things damaged or covered with cat saliva all the time.

WHY CATS WOOL SUCK

No one knows the actual reason why cats wool suck (the chewing and eating of clothing, especially wool), but there are various theories. One theory suggests that if kittens are taken away from their mothers too soon, the need to suckle gets transferred to other objects later in life. If your cat seems to be doing more sucking than chewing, and she kneads a blanket or piece of clothing with her paws while purring, this may be the case.

Another theory suggests that cats who wool suck need more fiber in their diets. If your cat has never done this before and begins to do so as an adult, especially if she swallows bits of the object, she must be stopped. It's possible that she is suffering from a medical problem such as parasites or an emotional problem such as stress or anxiety, so a visit to the vet is in order. Whatever the reason, wool

Wool sucking may originally stem from a nursing behavior that somehow became misdirected. Kittens taken away from their mothers too soon may transfer the need to suckle to other objects later in life.

sucking and chewing are unpleasant habits for anyone living with the aftereffects.

BREAKING THE HABIT

Although wool sucking and chewing are tough habits to break, it's not impossible to do so. Your first step should be to pick up all your clothes and anything your cat can destroy, and put those items out of reach behind closed doors and in drawers. Keep your cat out of the laundry room. (It's dangerous in there anyway because cats can climb into open dryers or ingest toxic laundry products.) Enforce a "no-cloth zone" because any relapse in your housekeeping will cause a relapse in wool sucking. If there are any areas in which this may be too difficult to accomplish, such as a bedroom where you have sheets, blankets, wardrobe, etc., be sure to keep those areas off-limits to your cat.

If those approaches don't seem adequate, you can always use a nontoxic spray repellant on the objects your cat seems particularly fond of whenever appropriate. An unpalatable solution of Bitter Apple or another type of antichewing solution will often work well as a deterrent.

Second, if your cat is fed canned food, switch to a dry food that's high in fiber, such as one that is specially made as a hairball formula. Cats on high-fiber diets often stop wool sucking if they are kept on this type of food. It's thought that the higher fiber intake takes the place of the wool that they crave in their diets.

Once your cat has been on the high-fiber diet and has gone a long time without touching clothing (a couple months), try giving her a single piece of fabric or a throwaway sock. If she shows no interest in your clothing, you might have broken her of the habit. Nevertheless, it's probably still a good idea to keep your kitty on her special diet and keep your clothes picked up.

SO NOW YOU KNOW...

- No one knows exactly what causes wool sucking, but it seems to be related to how young the cat was when she was taken from her mother. A kitten should not be removed from her mother until she is 12 weeks old.

Mommy Dearest

Because most cats who wool suck are often taken from their mothers too early, you may be wondering how old a kitten should be when you purchase her from a breeder or adopt her. Most kittens need to be with their moms until they're 12 weeks of age to ensure that they develop into healthy, well-adjusted adults.

You can help your cat break the wool-sucking habit by picking up all your clothes and anything your cat can destroy and putting those items out of reach behind closed doors and in closed drawers.

- Cats who wool suck should be put on a high-fiber diet, and all canned food should be eliminated.
- Keeping your clothing picked up and put away will help curb wool sucking.
- Putting an unpleasant tasting antichew solution or nontoxic repellant on items your cat likes to chew can work well as a deterrent.

Chewing Hazards

If your cat is a chewer, electrical cords can be a potential danger to her. Always keep her away from extension cords and outlets. Kittens, especially, may want to play with them. Keep them out of reach, or buy cord holders designed for use in homes with small children. You can also spray them with a nontoxic bitter spray to make them less appealing.

DANGEROUS CONSUMPTIVE BEHAVIOR

Wool sucking tends to be harmless to your cat if she does not ingest the material she sucks and chews on. However, some felines seem to have a compulsion to actually swallow or eat nonfood items, also known as pica. Although wool is the most commonly sought-after item, a few cats choose other fabrics or items such as human hair, plastic bags and objects, cardboard, or wood. Sometimes these items pass completely through the digestive system, but there is always the chance they could cause an intestinal obstruction. Over time, this compulsive habit could lead to the permanent damage of your cat's digestive system.

However, there are also a few health conditions such as diabetes or anemia that may cause this type of behavior, so it is always a good idea to have your cat examined by your veterinarian to rule out any medical issues. Contact your veterinarian right away if your cat develops diarrhea, vomiting, stops eating, or becomes lethargic.

If there was ever an animal who thought in multiple dimensions, it would be the cat. Felines have the almost magical quality of jumping higher and leaping greater distances than we humans expect. Unfortunately, sometimes that means that our inquisitive kitty friends can get into things they're not supposed to.

Chapter 11

Just Being Nosy: Counter Creeping and Other Boundary Issues

If there's an interesting smell, you can bet your cat will investigate it. If your cat is a mooch, she'll be up on the counter begging for tidbits while you cook. And don't forget that your stealthy feline knows when you're not home and will snoop in areas she normally wouldn't because you're not around to keep her out of trouble.

Here, we'll talk about the counter creeper and what can be done to keep her prying tendencies to a minimum.

WHY CATS SEEM TO GO EVERYWHERE

Cats are great pets, there's no doubt about that! But occasionally a kitty can be just a bit *too* nosy. She may always seem to get into things she shouldn't. Because cats can climb and jump with great skill, hopping up on a kitchen counter isn't a big deal for them. But it may be for you, especially if you're trying to cook dinner. It can be downright annoying to have a pesky pet who keeps lurking around the roast because she can't resist investigating every tempting aroma. But it can also be downright dangerous to have her accidentally hop up on a hot stove or to eat scraps of food that could make her sick from dirty dishes in the sink. Teaching your cat that these types of places are off-limits is vital to her overall safety—and there may be instances where it may save her life.

SETTING BOUNDARIES

You've probably noticed that cats go wherever they want to go. But in most cases, this occurs because you have allowed it to occur. As long as your cat doesn't

Foiled Again

Although some cats are deterred from going where they shouldn't by aluminum foil and odd nubby surfaces, many are not. Yet certain areas can be downright dangerous for them to walk on, such as a hot stove or an ironing board. In these circumstances, it may be crucial to take whatever measures necessary to ensure your cat's safety. If she hasn't responded to other deterrents, a small squirt of water on the rear end (never in the face!) is nothing compared to burnt paws—or worse. While use of this method isn't advocated on a regular basis, you may have to resort to drastic means if nothing else works to stop your curious cat from becoming injured.

have a deterrent, she'll go to any lengths to take a look at whatever catches her fancy. And yes, cats are indeed curious, so anything with an interesting smell is fair game to them.

To keep your kitty away from the areas you don't want her nosing around in, you're going to have to set boundaries. But before you do this, you must first have a good idea of what sort of boundaries you want to maintain. For example, do you want to keep your cat off your kitchen counters entirely or just when you are cooking? How about other areas of the house?

Believe it or not, you can set boundaries for your cat without too much effort. You simply have to be firm about where your cat is permitted to go and where she's not permitted to go, and *never* change the rules. Some cat owners use squirt bottles: Whenever their cat hops up on the counter, for instance, they gently squirt her with a spray of water on the rear end. The problem with doing this is that you must be there to correct the behavior whenever it occurs, otherwise your cat will only avoid the counter when you are home. However, some owners feel that this is not a very nice thing to do.

A better way to approach counter creeping is to use a reliable deterrent. As

Counter creepers are often motivated by their desire to investigate interesting smells.

discussed in previous chapters, you can use boundary-type devices to keep your cat away from off-limit areas. To review, these include:

- **SSSCAT:** Put this device on the floor near the counters. This is a practical deterrent because it won't inconvenience you by taking up work space on your counter.
- **Aluminum:** If your cat detests foil, putting some on your counter will discourage the behavior or at least make her jump off right away. Again, this method won't get in the way of your countertop needs.
- **Static mats:** For the more brazen and adventurous kitty who isn't challenged by foils or gusts of air, static mats placed on open counter space are more effective at keeping her away while you're gone.
- **Passive mats:** These are the mats with nubs on them; they make your counters really uncomfortable to walk on.

Obviously, if you need to use your entire kitchen counter space or you don't have much to begin with, you may have to resort to using several types of deterrents to support your needs at different times.

Setting firm boundaries is crucial to the safety and well-being of your cat.

Keeping Kitty Away From Human Food

Another good reason to use boundary training is to keep your cat away from food. Aside from the fact that most people don't particularly like their pets sampling their food, some of the items your kitty may nibble could be unhealthy or even toxic. Chocolate, onions, raisins, grapes, and undercooked and raw meat could pose serious health risks. And even if your cat doesn't eat foods that are dangerous for her, there are other hazards she may encounter. For example, she can burn herself on a hot stove or cut herself on a knife that you might have left out.

Obviously, the first thing to do is to teach your cat not to climb up on your counters in the first place. The second thing you'll need to do is to keep all food away from inquisitive noses, especially when you're not home. As they say, out of sight, out of mind. Many people use their microwaves and ovens to keep food out of a curious cat's reach when they're preparing meals. When not cooking, it's wise to return food to your refrigerator or cabinets right away. Some cats are quite adept at opening cabinets, however, so you may have to install childproof latches on them.

Keeping Kitty Away From Dog Food

Some cats like to eat dog food. Even though it might be tempting to allow your kitty to eat from your dog's bowl, it's not a good idea for several reasons. The main one is that she has special nutritional needs that are not completely addressed by dog food. Felines need more protein than dogs do, and they also require an amino acid called taurine, which is only found in meat. This is why it's important for your cat to eat a nutritionally balanced cat food.

But how do you keep your cat from eating your dog's food? The best way is not to free feed your dog. By free feeding, I mean leaving the bowl out all day so that your dog can nibble on it. Instead, put your dog on a feeding schedule. Plan to feed him first thing in the morning when you get up. Put his morning ration down where his free-feeding bowl would normally go, and show him his food. If you don't have a good idea of how much your dog should be eating in a single sitting, follow the manufacturer's instructions on the package or ask your veterinarian. Set a timer for 15 minutes. If, at the end of the 15 minutes, he hasn't eaten his food, pick up the bowl and

DID YOU KNOW?

Cats like eating dog food for a variety of reasons, but the main reason is because it is available and easily accessible. If the dog's kibble is just sitting there in the bowl, your cat figures it's fair game to eat because it smells a bit like cat food and comes in pellet form. Of course, your feline should not eat dog food because it isn't nutritionally balanced for cats, so always remove the bowl as soon as your dog has finished eating.

Avoid Potpourri

For some reason, cats find liquid potpourri to be quite tempting—the smell must be intoxicating to them. However, they seem to be more sensitive to these items than other pets. Not only can the hot liquid burn your cat, but many of the ingredients are irritating to her respiratory tract or can be toxic to her. If you must have potpourri, use it in rooms where there is no chance your kitty can get at it. You can also substitute relatively safer air fresheners such as plug-ins or unlit candles on warming trays to provide a lovely, more cat-friendly fragrance.

put the food away. (If it's canned food, you may have to put it in the refrigerator until the next meal). Do the same thing again in the evening.

You'll have to be sure that your cat doesn't mug your dog for his food. A good way to do this is to feed your cat at the same time as your dog but in a different place. Choose a location your cat can get to but your dog can't. Many people feed their cat in a different room. That way, she won't feel stressed and can eat her meal without interruption.

SO NOW YOU KNOW...

- Cats counter creep because they are investigating tempting smells.
- You can keep your cat off the countertops by using both passive and active deterrents, such as aluminum foil and static mats, to keep them off.
- Some human foods may be toxic to your cat. Know which foods are unsafe for her, and keep them out of reach at all times.
- Don't let your cat have access to dog food. Felines have different nutritional requirements than dogs do, so dog food is never a healthy replacement for appropriate cat food.
- Setting firm boundaries is crucial to the safety and well-being of your cat.

Some of the items your kitty may nibble, such as certain human foods, could be unhealthy or even toxic.

HOLIDAY HAZARDS

Oddly enough, the most perfect kitty becomes naughty, not nice, during the holidays. And whether you celebrate Christmas, Hanukkah, Kwanzaa, or any other holiday around the winter solstice, you can guarantee that the accoutrement of the season is going to attract your cat's attention. Look at it the way she sees it: Suddenly your entire house has been transformed into one big, enticing cat toy. There are fragrant candles, cookies and treats, wrapped presents with bows and strings, tinsel, garland, shiny ornaments, and let's not forget that giant cat tree! (And the live ones smell unbelievably good to your scent-loving feline.) It's a feast of things to explore, sniff, and chew. So what should you do? You can't have one tree for yourself and one just for your cat.

Well, around the holidays, both of you are going to have to make some concessions. To keep life sane, with minimal damage to your cat and your home, take the following precautions:

- Put away all those lovely, breakable ornaments. You know, those heirlooms your grandma gave you. Likewise, don't use icicle tinsel on your tree, and keep tinsel garlands far from your cat's reach. Don't display lit candles.

- Keep your cat out of the room in which you have displayed your holiday decorations unless you are there to supervise her. Cats have been known to climb trees and skate down them while their owners aren't looking, destroying everything on the tree and possibly getting hurt. Set boundaries around your decorations—especially your tree—if necessary.

- Keep electrical cords out of your cat's reach, or spray them with a bitter spray. One bite could spell disaster.

- Don't display mistletoe, holly, lilies, or other dangerous plants. Check out the ASPCA's list of dangerous plants at www.aspca.org.

- Place a scratcher or a planter of catnip near the holiday tree.

As is the case any time of the year, setting firm boundaries for your cat is vital to keeping her out of trouble and safe from the possibility of injury or death.

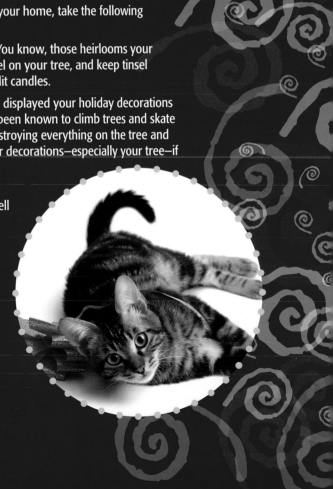

Your cat brings you presents. Unfortunately, they're the gross, icky variety in the form of dead mice and other animals. And they're not cleanly killed either. They have their heads bitten off, or maybe they're in bits and pieces (yikes!). Or maybe all that you're given is a mouse tail. It's gross and disgusting, and you want it to stop.

Mmmm, Good: Bringing in Mousey

WHY YOUR CAT HUNTS

If you've never had a cat or if you've never had a cat who has hunted, you may be surprised to hear that despite your cat's domestication and the fact that she is regularly fed, she still likes to hunt. Even when well fed, many cats will chase small animals and kill them. It's a natural instinct that has served cats well for thousands of years.

Think about it. Domestication took place about 10,000 years ago. The cat became domesticated on her terms, not ours. Humans invited her to stay so that she would hunt mice and other vermin to keep our grain free from rodents and their disease-carrying parasites. Until recently, her job was primarily to kill mice!

Cat's are predatory carnivores; therefore, the urge to hunt is a natural instinct that even domestic cats will display.

Cats are predators. They are carnivores, meaning that they need to eat meat to survive. In the wild, they kill small animals such as mice, rats, birds, and even small bunnies if given the opportunity. They chase and play with their prey, wearing it down so that they can kill it with a minimal amount of harm to themselves. All of this behavior is completely natural, even if we humans find their actions cruel or inhumane.

When you play with your cat using a feather or teaser toy, you're essentially

tapping into these natural instincts. Batting around a rubber mouse and chasing after a toy on a string are nothing short of hunting behaviors. You'll notice that cats love things that make erratic movements and will chase toys much more if you play with them in this manner. These movements simulate how mice scurry along, especially when being pursued. Your cat finds the chase exciting because it stimulates her drive to stalk and hunt. Aside from keeping her skills sharp, your kitty enjoys playing with you in this way. Also, the mental and physical activity helps alleviate boredom, keeps her healthy, and strengthens the bond between you.

WHY YOUR CAT BRINGS YOU A MOUSE (OR BITS THEREOF)

Okay, so you understand that your cat hunts because it's completely natural to her—it's like breathing or eating. But what about bringing you the mouse or the leftovers?

Toxic Mice

You probably know that mouse and rat poisons are dangerous to your cat if she ingests them, but do you know that if your cat consumes part of a mouse that has ingested the poison, it could kill her, too? Just because the poison has been metabolized in the mouse doesn't mean that it is any less toxic.

Never use poisons, snap-type traps, or glue boards to kill mice. Instead, consider using humane traps that are safe to have around pets so that your cat won't have an unfortunate incident with one.

Well, there are several theories behind this. The first theory has to do with your place in your cat's life: She sees you as the top alpha cat, and she's paying respect by sharing her kill. You may notice that after your kitty deposits her gift, she meows to get your attention and your approval. That's pretty cool, if you think about it.

The second theory, in my opinion, is more probable and a bit more amusing. Your cat has figured out that you're not such a great hunter, and like any good momma cat, she's going to show you how to hunt. So she starts by bringing you bits of "food" or even whole dead mice. Then, if you're really lucky (as lucky as I've been), she'll bring you stunned mice to help you learn to kill your own prey. (Imagine her horror when you fail to kill the mouse the way she expected you would.)

While you may not be appreciative of her presents, your cat has actually given you a bit of a compliment by trying to feed you and care for you. So when you receive your next headless mouse, consider it a compliment and just dispose of it when she's not looking.

KEEP YOUR CAT FROM HUNTING?!

What if you don't want your cat to hunt? If you have mice indoors (like I sometimes do), you're out of luck. Your cat is going to hunt them no matter what you do. She's probably more effective than those mousetraps you've set up anyway. Once the mice are gone, your cat won't have anything to hunt. Problem solved.

If you still want to help rid your house of those squeaky uninvited visitors, don't use poison or traps that can harm your cat or other animals. Mouse poison can hurt or kill a cat if she ingests it or if she eats a mouse that has ingested it. If you decide to set traps, use humane ones and put them in areas your cat won't have access to so that she doesn't get hurt.

But what about your indoor/outdoor cat who brings in birds, mice, or rats? Well, because you can't control your cat when she is wandering outside, the best thing to do is to keep her *inside*. That way, your cat won't have the opportunity to hunt wild prey, and she'll be safer anyway.

Other ways you can discourage your cat from hunting include feeding her adequately so that she doesn't wander around still feeling hungry and looking for an extra snack. A bell attached to a collar is a good way to warn any prey in the area of your cat's presence, although that may be a little frustrating for your cat.

All this being said, the best way to prevent this behavior from becoming a big problem at home is to keep your cat busy. Offer her a variety of toys to chase and regular playtime with you so that she can derive all the satisfaction she needs from simulating the hunt.

Although you can never really stop your cat from hunting, you can discourage the behavior by providing her with a variety of toys to chase so that she can derive all the satisfaction she needs from simulating the hunt.

SO NOW YOU KNOW...

- Cats are predators, so hunting mice and small prey is a basic instinct.
- Your cat is bringing you dead mice (or bits thereof) to feed you because she wants you to learn how to hunt.
- If you have an indoor/outdoor cat, she will continue to hunt and bring you dead animals. Keeping her indoors is the only way to stop this.
- If you have mice indoors, your cat will probably hunt them.
- Don't use poison or traps that can hurt your cat. Use only humane traps that are approved for use around pets. Also, mice that have died from ingesting poison can still be toxic to your cat if she eats them. Use other methods to capture mice.
- The best way to prevent this behavior from becoming a big problem at home is to keep your cat busy by offering her a variety of toys and regular playtime with you.

HUNTING GAMES

Cats are highly specialized hunters. They are known to hunt more than 1,000 species for food. Skilled and effective predators, their style of hunting uses short bursts of intense energy followed by long periods of rest. Domestic felines ambush or pounce upon and immobilize their prey much in the same way their big cat relatives do in the wild. This predatory behavior is a characteristic that all cats are born with, so you're not going to be able to keep your kitty from doing it. They learn it from their mothers, who teach them how to trap, kill, and eat prey when they are kittens.

Not surprisingly, domestic cats, especially kittens, are known for their love of play. As you probably know, most cats can't resist a dangling piece of string or a rubber mouse wiggled enticingly across the floor. That's because these toys fuel your cat's natural hunting instincts by mimicking moving prey. However, when cats live in domestic environments where there is no prey available to chase and kill, they tend to express their hunting instincts by chasing imaginary prey. You might see your cat running around the house, leaping about and pouncing on things, hanging onto your curtains, or maybe even stalking people and imagining them as their prey. By offering your mighty hunter a variety of toys and regular playtime with you, you can keep this behavior from becoming a problem at home. As cats get older, they may become bored or put off by the effort required to do all that stalking and pouncing, so the behavior will occur less often or not at all.

You're exhausted from a long day at work. You have a presentation in the morning, and you need a good night's sleep. You drink a cup of chamomile tea, set the alarm, and crawl into bed. No sooner have the lights gone out do you hear your cat playing with her toys. She's bouncing around the house like a five-year-old who defiantly refuses to take a nap.

Working the Night Shift: Nocturnal Hyperactivity

She's pouncing on you, too, even nibbling at your ears and toes. Suddenly, you think that this whole pet thing may not be such a wonderful idea. But discovering the reasons behind a cat's nocturnal tendencies may help you keep your kitty less active at night.

WHY CATS INSIST ON PLAYING AT NIGHT

So what gives? Why is your cat racing around after the lights go out? And is there any way for you to curb her nighttime antics? Well, first of all, you must understand that cats are mostly nocturnal creatures whose prey comes out at night. In the wild, they sleep most of the day (after all, that's what cats do) are rested and raring to go in the evening, when their prey shows up.

Because play is just another form of hunting to your housecat, she is wide awake and active after nightfall. She doesn't understand that you need a good night's rest, and chances are she is a bit confused by your behavior. After all, she's awake, so why aren't you?

WEARING KITTY OUT BEFORE BEDTIME

How do you get a good night's sleep when your kitty insists on bouncing about so madly? The work starts *before* you go to bed, preferably in the early evening when you both still have plenty of energy. You'll have to engage in these daily play sessions for quite a while for the training to work. Here's how to begin.

During dinnertime, give your kitty some toys so that she can be entertained while you make and eat dinner. Choose some of her favorite items, and nestle them in catnip for a day or two so that they'll smell fresh and interesting when you give them to your cat. If she is a catnip junkie, they will smell like heaven to her and she won't be able to resist playing with them. Even if your cat doesn't react to catnip, the scent will make the toys smell new and fresh. Most cats love playing with new toys, so giving her the old ones disguised as new ones works well. Let her play with those for a bit.

When you're done with dinner, pull out the teasers and fishing toys and play together. (You can do this while watching television.) Continue playing with your kitty until

DID YOU KNOW?

Although cats are crepuscular by nature, which is to say they are most active during dawn and dusk, they are mostly night hunters because that's when their prey is out and about.

Their eyesight is so good at night that they can see in near pitch blackness, and the shape of their pupils allows them to expand for maximum sight in the dark.

she isn't interested anymore, and then take a break. Resume play when you think that she may be in the mood again. Do this throughout the evening until you go to bed. Both you and your cat will enjoy the interaction, and it'll be a fun way to wind down the day.

How you play with your cat is important, too. You need to play with her as though the toy is an actual prey item. (Only use teaser toys and fishing toys on poles to keep her from clawing you.) If you move the toy around as if it's a mouse or a wounded bird, your cat will go crazy over it. Let her "catch" the toy occasionally, and let her carry it off for a bit before starting to play again.

Once it's time to go to bed, wind down the play session by allowing your cat to catch the toy more often. Then put all the toys away, and let your cat settle down quietly for a while. She will appreciate the signal that it's time to quit and will most likely be tired from all that evening activity. After all that wonderful bonding time, your cat will most certainly appreciate snuggling in bed.

The best way to limit your cat's late-night activities is to play with her before bedtime.

Resetting the Clock

Basically, all this early evening activity helps reset your kitty's sleep clock so that you can enjoy a good night's rest. How long will this take? It depends a lot on your cat, really, but I would continue play training for at least two months before cutting it back to a session or two just before bedtime. You never know, though; you and your cat may enjoy this time together so much that you make it a nightly ritual long after your cat has decided that going to bed early might be better.

If you have more than one cat, you can guarantee that there's going to be a bit of night action going on when your cats aren't sleepy. Playing with both cats and getting them to have a good romp before you go to bed is one way to ensure that they are a bit less active.

WHAT TO DO WHEN KITTY IS NOISY

Even if you engage in regular play training, you may occasionally still have to cope with a noisy nocturnal cat. There are a few things you can do. The first is to keep your cat inside the bedroom with the door closed so that she gets the idea that it's time to settle down and go to sleep. Of course, that would be the ideal scenario.

However, if your nocturnal ninja kitty continues to disturb you during the night or she scratches at the door and yowls to get out, you may have to keep her out of the bedroom and confine her to another room far enough away that her nighttime antics won't disturb you. Providing her with a comfortable sleeping area and a nearby litter box may do the trick. If she remains awake, consider providing ample opportunity for scratching, climbing, and play, which can keep her occupied until she tuckers out. It's also a good idea to pick up all her noisy toys—the ones with the bells and squeaky parts—and put them away before retiring for the evening so that your cat won't have an incentive to play with them while everyone else is sleeping (or trying to sleep). You may still need to use the typical deterrent devices such as SSSCAT and static mats to keep your cat away from your bedroom door or away from other interesting stuff that's off-limits.

The Wake-Up Call

Every morning at the crack of dawn you're peacefully asleep, and your cat either pounces on you or begins yowling incessantly. You've tried ignoring her, but that doesn't work. And when you've shut the door and kept her out of the bedroom, she just scratches at it and yowls even louder. It's getting so that you can't get a good night's rest.

But your cat can't help waking up when she does, and once she's up, she wants you to be up, too. Besides, her biological clock is different than yours. So what can you do? Well, if you feed your cat first thing when you get up, you will find that she rouses you from sleep much earlier than you'd like because she expects to be fed her breakfast. Try providing meals only after your morning is well underway if you can. Also, before you retire for the evening, provide her with plenty of toys to keep her occupied before you get up. If you continue to ignore her morning nagging, she may just give up and resort to other activities.

If your cat doesn't take well to being confined in your bedroom during the night, set up another location where she can play and be active without disturbing you.

SO NOW YOU KNOW...

- Cats stay up at night to hunt and therefore to play as well.
- Plan and encourage play and feeding during daytime and evening hours so that your cat's schedule more closely matches yours.
- You can tire your cat out with play sessions before she goes to bed. Discourage catnaps during the evening.
- Having your cat sleep with you in your bedroom with the door closed may help reset her sleep clock and let her know that it's time to settle down and go to bed.
- If your cat doesn't take well to being confined in your bedroom, set up another location where she can play and be active during the night without disturbing you.
- If all else fails, you can always resort to earplugs!

Meow, meow, meow. You should've named your cat Chatty Kitty instead. She meows all the time—when you feed her, when she greets you, and when she wants attention. It's getting on your nerves. Can you actually get your cat to be less chatty?

Chapter 14

Can You Hear Me Now?: Mouthy Cats

Exploring why cats meow will not only tell you a lot about what your cat is thinking but can help you deal with an excessively mouthy cat more effectively.

WHY YOUR CAT MEOWS

You may be wondering why cats meow. Obviously, cats use vocalizations as a form of communication, but they don't use it as a language in the way that we do. In fact, oddly enough, feral cats don't do a lot of meowing, nor do cats in the wild. Meowing seems to be more connected with the attempts of domestic cats to get attention from their humans.

Cats are very smart creatures. While they use a variety of ways to communicate with each other—body position, scents, and vocalizations—they have watched humans and determined that we're a little clueless about picking up on pheromones and feline body language. No doubt cats have figured out that a human's main form of communication is vocal because we respond when someone talks to us. So they learned to meow to us to tell us what they want and need.

Extremely intelligent creatures, cats have figured out that a human's main form of communication is vocal, so they learned to meow to tell us what they want and need.

Kitty Chitchat

Cats have a wide range of vocalizations—from meows and mews to hisses and purrs. Scientists believe that they actually produce more than 100 different vocalizations, but experts cannot agree on how a cat purrs. Some scientists speculate that cats purr through a set of false vocal chords, while others think that muscle contractions in the chest are responsible for the sound. Experts also do not know exactly why cats purr or what it means. Cats purr when they are happy, relaxed, and content, yet they also purr when they are hurt or stressed. Some breeds of cat are very vocal and love to talk, while others are less chatty.

But cats also have plenty of nonvocal communications such as body posture; ear, tail, skin, and facial movements; and pheromone (scent) communications. Some owners instinctively know what their cat is thinking or feeling based on the flick of an ear or the twitch of the tail. These owners have learned their cat's body language. Understanding your cat is the best way to work out problem behaviors, but more importantly, it's a good way to develop a strong relationship, build trust, and form a lifelong bond.

Some breeds of cat are mouthier than others. Oriental breeds are usually a lot more vocal than other cats, so it's natural for them to meow more.

HOW TO REDUCE THE MEOWING

Your cat vocalizes because you've reacted to her meows in the past, and they've gotten her what she wanted. So let's say that your cat constantly bugs you to open the bedroom door in the wee hours of the morning, and you're tired of having to get up before your alarm clock goes off. The best way to approach this problem is to ignore your cat while she is meowing. Then, when she is finally silent, you can open the door.

The problem with taking this tack is that sometimes your cat will try to get your attention by meowing longer and louder. It's not unlike a person who is trying to speak in English to someone who doesn't know the language. The individual may speak louder and more slowly to get the other person to understand. Your cat thinks that maybe you've misunderstood, so she tries harder to communicate in an attempt to get you to do what she wants. In the end, you both may become very frustrated.

Your cat vocalizes because you've reacted to her meows in the past, so the easiest way to deal with a mouthy cat is to ignore her until she stops meowing.

Another option you might try is clicker training. With the clicker, you can substitute a less vocal behavior for the meowing. To do this, you'll have to teach the clicker and the target stick. (See Chapter 2.) Once you have that established, the next step is to teach your cat that meowing will not produce the desired results, but another behavior will.

Begin training by choosing a time when your cat isn't meowing at you for something. For example, if she constantly meows at you to open the bedroom door during the night, use the training when she is in the vicinity of a door but not asking to be let in or out. You will need to use the clicker and target stick to lure your cat over to the door, so have them available, and be ready to take advantage of these opportunities as they come up. When your cat approaches a closed door, click and treat her. Then, have her sit and wait at the door. When she does so, click and open the door. She may be surprised by this and immediately check out the room, or she may wait for another treat. If so, give it to her. Once she comes out of the room and is back where she started, close the door and repeat the exercise. Eventually, you will be able to eliminate the treat and the clicker.

Until you feel that the behavior has been modified, though, try to keep your doors closed so that you have ample opportunity to practice the training. Whenever your cat meows to come in or go out, ignore it and instead get your clicker and target stick and repeat the entire exercise.

The clicker works when training for good behavior in other situations as well. For example, you can use it to stop your cat from meowing excessively around her mealtime or during your dinner. By substituting another appropriate behavior for the problem one, you're teaching your cat good manners, and in this case, teaching her to make less noise.

SO NOW YOU KNOW...

- Cats meow largely to get human attention.
- Some breeds of cat talk more than others.
- You can reduce the frequency of meows by not reacting to them.
- You can teach an alternative, more appropriate behavior to meowing by using the clicker.

Hypervocalization

You'll never completely get your cat to be quiet. If you have a low tolerance for constant kitty chitchat, don't get a breed that has a predilection for being a talker, such as Siamese and other Oriental breeds.

The most common cause for hypervocalization is that meowing for attention has become a learned behavior—your kitty has always gotten what she wanted if she meowed at you long enough—although fear and anxiety can also be responsible. Other causes could stem from biological reasons such as hunger, pain, estrus, or medical conditions.

Chapter 15

Going Places: Travel Phobia

Occasionally, you're going to need to take your cat out. I'm not talking about taking her to a cat park or the shopping mall; I'm talking about taking her to the vet or to a boarding kennel. If you show your cat or participate in an activity like agility, you'll need to take her on the road to various events, which will most likely involve an extended stay away from home. And what if you're moving? How do you prepare your cat for that?

Anyone who has taken a kitty on a trip, be it short or long, knows that cats can become absolutely frantic when riding in a car. In fact, they don't much like leaving their territory. They are happier staying at home. Nevertheless, there are steps you can take to make traveling more comfortable for your feline friend—it just takes a little preparation and some training.

CATS ARE HOMEBODIES

So why *are* cats so stressed when you want to take them out and about? To understand their anxiety, you must first look at their very nature. Cats are essentially homebodies. They don't like to leave their established territory, whether it's a home, a particular alley, or an empty field. In the wild, cats will leave their territory only if forced to do so, either because hunting isn't good or because other cats or predators have forced them to move on.

You may recall that cats were domesticated when humans finally became agrarian. The grain in the fields and storage sheds attracted mice and rats. Local cats decided that it was a good idea to hang around these humans because it was easy to find and hunt vermin. There's no doubt that cats moved along with humans to take advantage of the abundant sources of food and protection, but they did so cautiously and slowly. No doubt the early humans found cats useful and decided to bring them along as they moved from place to place. Still, I suspect that the first domestic cats found travel as disconcerting as our modern feline companions do.

Basically, cats don't appear to like new experiences, and they would be far happier if they never had to deal with changing environments. But that doesn't mean that you can't train them to get beyond their basic instincts and become accustomed to being on the move.

In the wild, cats will leave their territory only if forced to do so, either because hunting isn't good or because other cats or predators have forced them to move on.

TRAINING YOUR CAT FOR TRAVEL

Training a cat for travel should start when she is a kitten. Simple things such as trips to the vet and a visit to a friend's home will make all the difference between having a comfortable traveler and a scaredy

There's No Place Like Home

There's an evolutionary reason to explain why cats prefer to stay at home. From the biggest cats to the smallest ones, the main reason is that they want to make sure that there are enough prey species and resources to adequately support them in the wild. Cats carve out their territories because it will ensure their survival and also because it will ensure that they don't have to fight with competitors all the time. Problems in catdom generally occur when prey is scarce or when there is a new cat on the block. With the exception of lions, cats are solitary hunters.

That being said, feral cats do seem to tolerate each other in feral cat colonies. Although they can still have their own zones, some social bonding does occur. This probably happened as a result of a lack of resources and because there were too many cats forced into a small area, especially in cities.

cat. Early life is the most important time in a cat's development, a phase during which she is learning through experimentation, just like a human child. Therefore, this is the best time to shape appropriate behaviors and to start training her, although you can still teach an old cat new tricks too if you use the right approach.

Carrier Training

To prepare your cat for travel, you'll need to teach her to accept being confined in a travel carrier. You can do this by getting her used to sleeping in it. To make the experience as positive as possible, give her all possible comforts. Put soft material inside the carrier, such as a towel or small blanket, and spray the inside with feline pheromones to make it more welcoming. Help her associate the carrier with good feelings by speaking softly to her and playing with a favorite toy, first near the carrier and then when she is inside of it. Next, try closing the door briefly. If your cat panics, open the door right away and resume training another day.

Repeat this entire exercise until your cat becomes more comfortable inside the carrier with the door closed. Eventually, she will know what to expect, and she will begin to relax a bit. When she seems reasonably content inside the carrier, close the door and walk away for a few minutes. Then return and open the door. Do this for a few days, leaving her alone for longer periods. Don't make a fuss, even if she cries. After each training session, make sure that she has plenty of playtime and attention outside the carrier. Always end training on a positive note. With patience and positive reinforcement, your kitty will adjust to the carrier in no time and may even come to think of it as her special place.

Types of Carriers

Ideally, you should have at least two types of carriers. One carrier should be used for car trips, and aside from containing your kitty, it should be big enough to comfortably hold bedding, food and water dishes, and a small litter box. The carrier should also fit in your car with no hassle. It's a good idea to have a soft-sided travel carrier as well. These are good for shorter trips or for air travel because they are much more cat-friendly than the hard plastic carriers the airlines provide. This carrier should fit under the seat in an aircraft. (Check with the airlines before making travel arrangements to be sure that you can use a soft-sided carrier to carry your cat onboard.)

LOW-STRESS CAR TRIPS

Your cat's first trips away from home should be as stress-free as possible. Visits to a friend's house (which should be planned in advance so that your cat can't

Flying Cats

Cats can indeed fly the friendly skies, but before you take off for the airport, you're going to have to do some research. Airlines require that health certificates be presented for each pet ten days before travel. Every airline has its own rules and regulations, whether you are carrying your pet onboard or keeping her in the cargo hold, which may be mandatory. This is why it's so important to contact the airline to confirm its policies. Some airlines charge for bringing a pet onboard, even if you stow her under the seat in front of you. Plan accordingly so that your feline companion won't be stranded at the airport.

Keep in mind that airline rules are constantly changing due to security issues or other special circumstances. Always contact the airline you are flying for the latest regulations so that both you and your kitty can have a safe and uneventful flight.

escape if she gets nervous) or just a quick ride in the car followed by a reward once she's back home will help get her used to the idea that traveling isn't so bad. Always make these "test runs" short and uneventful—your cat will appreciate it.

Also, never allow your cat to ride loose in the car. A travel carrier will prevent your panicked cat from causing an accident because she won't be able to get underfoot or escape through an open window. Spray the carrier with feline pheromones to help keep her calm.

Training for Car Rides

Again, if you want to train your cat to calmly accept riding in the car, it's best to begin when she's young. Positive reinforcement is the key here, as it is in every training situation. Use favorite foods or toys to keep her distracted and content during travel. Of course, she should always be in her carrier while you are in transit. During the early stages of training, you can also have someone your cat trusts (such as another family member) sit next to her and reassure her by offering her goodies through the carrier door. Gradually extend the time she spends in the car until she can associate the experience with something that isn't stressful or scary. Plan to spend some quality time with her after every trip so that she knows she is guaranteed her previous affection and sense of security.

Make your trips short and fun. If they are always positive and upbeat, there's a good chance that your cat will relax and accept riding in the car without too much stress.

PREPARING FOR TRAVEL

When traveling with your cat, bring along everything she will need while she's away, both to provide for her comfort and to prevent problem behaviors caused by travel issues. Stick to her regular routine as closely as possible. She will not become anxious or stressed if feeding and playtime still occur at their usual times. Set aside a few minutes each day to give her extra attention. The more she feels "at home" while traveling, the more relaxed she'll be.

Identification

Before you go anywhere, you must put some form of identification on your cat.

First, put an identification tag on her collar that shows all her pertinent information (name, address, your contact information). These tags are typically inexpensive and available through your veterinarian, by mail order, or purchased from a pet-supply store. There are even vending machines that can provide you with a nice shiny tag within minutes if need be.

If your cat doesn't have a collar, you can purchase one at most department stores or at any pet-supply store. Just make sure that it's a breakaway collar, meaning that if your cat snags it on something, it will open easily so that she won't choke to death. The positive aspect of this type of collar is obvious—it will save your cat's life. The negative aspect is that once the collar comes off, there's no way to identify your cat. This leads us to the subject of microchips.

Without some form of permanent ID, you may never locate your missing cat. However, if she gets implanted with a microchip, she can be identified and quickly reunited with you. Microchips are not much bigger than a grain of rice, and they are a painless and permanent form of identification. Your veterinarian will inject the microchip just below the skin between the shoulder blades. The procedure causes a brief

Travel Caution

Although you probably know this already, it bears repeating: Never leave your cat alone in the car, especially during warm and hot weather. Cars can heat up rapidly, even with the windows down, and your cat can suffer heatstroke rather quickly. Cold can also be a serious problem for your cat, so plan accordingly. If you need to make multiple stops or you will be out of the car for a long period, it may be best to leave her at home.

amount of discomfort, one which is quickly forgotten and well worth it in the long run.

Once your cat is microchipped, she can be registered with a national database. In the event that she is found, the facility to which she is taken can scan and read the information on the chip. The veterinarian or shelter can then contact the appropriate pet registry, which in turn will look up your pet's file on the database (name, address, owner's contact information, etc.) and call you to make arrangements for your pet's safe return home.

Well, at least that's how it works in theory. In reality, the shelter or veterinarian must have the ability to read the chip. Although pet ID chips haven't been standardized yet, many of the manufacturers are moving toward providing a standardized reader. The owner must also keep her pet registered with the registry organization (which simply entails paying a one-time fee) and update the contact information when necessary.

Although there are still some problems with this system, it's certainly better to use a method that works most of the time than to have a lost pet who has no possibility of being identified.

While away from home, visible identification tags can save your cat's life if she becomes lost.

PACKING FOR YOUR CAT

When traveling with your cat, you need to have certain supplies on hand so that the trip can go smoothly. Your cat has daily needs and comforts, just as you do. More importantly, you want her to remain healthy and safe while she's away from home. Even cats are vulnerable to the uncertainties and perils of travel.

The Basics

Cats hate change, and this applies to their environment and diet. You're not the only one who may suffer digestive upset or insomnia during travel. Bring all these basic items along to ensure her well-being:

- **A cat carrier:** The size of the carrier your cat needs will depend on whether you travel via airplane or car. When traveling by plane, a carrier that fits under the seat is best. When riding in a car, a carrier that can carry food, water, and a litter box is best.

- **Collar and ID tags:** As you already know, this is an absolute must.
- **Walking harness and leash:** These are important for those times when you might not be able to have your cat in the carrier or she must be out of the car in an unsafe area, such as a rest stop.
- **Vaccination and health records:** If you're flying, you'll need a health certificate signed by a veterinarian. Even if you're driving, having health and vaccination records on hand can help your cat in emergency situations.
- **Food and water dishes**: You should always bring food for at least 24 hours more than you expect to be away from home. Your cat may not eat unfamiliar food, especially if she suffers any kind of digestive upset from

When Medication Is Necessary

You've tried to get your cat to tolerate travel, but she hates it. As a result, you've resigned yourself to the fact that you're just never going to be able to take her anywhere.

But let's face it: There are times when you absolutely have to take your cat on the road. The obvious necessity might be a trip to the vet's office, although you may be able to get around that if you have access to a mobile veterinary service. In most cases, a mobile vet can come to your home and do most of the work there. But even a trip to the vet is minor if her office isn't far away. I'm talking about going cross-country with your cat because you're moving or because you're going to be away from home for an extended period.

If you must travel by car or airplane with a cat who is too freaked out to handle the trip, talk with your veterinarian. She can prescribe medications that will help calm and control your pet. It's not the best solution, but it may be the only solution if your cat can't travel any other way.

it. This will make travel unpleasant for both you and your cat. In extreme cases, such as times when there might be bad weather, you may need food for several days. Plan accordingly. Also, if you are flying, check with the airlines to see if you need food and water dishes that snap onto the carrier. (These are often required.)

- **A pet first-aid kit:** Mishaps can occur on the road, so be prepared to offer your cat the assistance she may need until you can get her to a vet.
- **Travel litter box and litter:** Finicky about most things, these are items your cat may not be willing to compromise on at all—don't take that chance.
- **Enzymatic cleaner and towels:** These are good to bring along for those occasional accidents.
- **Bedding, toys, teasers, and portable scratchers:** While these are optional, your cat will appreciate your thoughtfulness, and they will help give her a greater sense of security.

HITTING THE ROAD: THE RULES OF TRAVEL

You've made all the necessary preparations and arrangements, and you're ready to hit the road. As you embark on your journey, remember that your feline companion's safety is of the utmost importance. Contain your cat in a safe and secure place at all times—whether on the road or in your lodgings. Otherwise, you run the risk of her getting loose and becoming lost in strange and unfamiliar surroundings. And I can guarantee that situation won't be fun for either of you.

When planning a stay at a hotel, be sure that the establishment accepts cats (many don't) before making your reservation. In some cases, the hotel will charge an additional fee to allow for extra cleaning and for possible damage the pet may cause. While it may seem that you are being unfairly taken advantage of as a pet owner, the reality is that some pets have caused problems in the past and the hotel or motel owners are just protecting their interests.

Whatever you do, don't try to sneak your cat in with you. Hotels workers can quickly figure out that a pet has been in the room—and then you'll be faced with extra costs and maybe even an eviction.

Hotel Pet Etiquette

Never leave your cat loose in the room while you're out. Housekeeping or other maintenance workers may accidentally let her escape (not knowing that you have a cat loose in the room), or your cat may feel stressed by the invading strangers and do damage by clawing the furniture, spraying, or possibly scratching the unfamiliar

What if My Cat *Really* Hates to Travel?

If you're only going to be away from home for a day or two, you can leave your cat home alone provided that you have a timed feeder. However, cats will become bored and lonely without companionship, human or otherwise. So if you're going to be gone longer than that, ask a friend or neighbor to visit periodically and check on your kitty. She can play with her, make sure that she has enough food and water, and tend to the litter box. Having a friend or neighbor check in will be a load off your mind as well.

visitor. Although putting a sign on the door may or may not alert hotel workers, you're still taking a risk leaving your cat uncrated without adequate supervision.

During your hotel stay, put the litter box and food dishes in the bathroom, where it's easy to clean up any mess. If your cat likes to sleep with you at night, you may wish to bring your own blanket to lay on top of the bed so that her hair doesn't stick to the bedding. The next guests using the room may be allergic to cats, so be conscientious. If you take your cat outside of the room, be sure that she is wearing a cat harness she can't wriggle out of, and keep her on a leash. This is to protect her while being courteous to the other guests. Your other option is to transport her in a soft carrier to ensure her safety.

Last, be aware that you're visiting a hotel that has graciously allowed your pet to stay with you. This is not an entitlement—it's a privilege. Clean up accidents wherever they occur, and leave your hotel room in better condition than you found it.

HOME ALONE

Depending on your cat's age and temperament, it might be a lot less stressful for her to remain at home when you decide to travel for an extended period. So if you're going on vacation or a business trip for a week or more, you may want to hire a professional pet sitter to care for your cat, or if that's not possible, you may want to consider boarding her.

Pet Sitters

There are a number of organizations that can refer you to a cat-loving, trained professional in your area. Your veterinarian may be able to recommend several pet sitters whom her clients have used before. You can also locate a reputable sitter by contacting the National Association of Professional Pet Sitters (NAPPS) at www. petsitters.org.

If you've opted to try a sitter, never hire anyone for whom you're unable to get references or recommendations, and make sure that the person or business you've selected is insured. Arrange to meet the professional who will be taking care of your cat, and introduce them to each other to see if they get along. If your cat takes an immediate liking to the person, it's a good sign; if she despises her on sight, you may need to make other arrangements.

Most cats don't like changes in their routine, so the best solution when you travel may be to leave your feline at home and enlist the services of a pet sitter.

Your chosen pet sitter should like and understand cats. Whenever possible, choose someone your cat knows and trusts. Leave specific written instructions about feeding times, the amount of food to feed, the general schedule, and any medications she may need. Give the pet sitter the name, address, and phone number of the vet's office, as well as directions to the office. Also, leave a contact number where you can be reached in case of an emergency. Have enough cat food and litter on hand to last through the duration of your absence.

Boarding

Another option to consider if you are planning to be away for awhile is boarding your cat at a pet boarding facility. Ask friends and neighbors for recommendations, and research the various establishments. Visit several boarding kennels before making a final decision, and always ask for a tour.

The kennel should look and smell clean, fresh water should be available, and the litter boxes should be relatively unsoiled. Don't hesitate to ask specific questions about the qualifications of the workers, the number of cats being boarded, and their procedures in the event of a veterinary emergency. Your veterinarian's office may also board cats or may be able to give you several recommendations for reputable places in your area.

Today, there are many modern "cat-only" kennels and boarding facilities that exclusively board cats in a cozy, home-like setting. Often referred to as "pet hotels," these facilities employ qualified people to feed, groom, and play with your kitty throughout her stay.

Many owners still prefer to leave their cat at home with a pet sitter or a friend rather than board them in a strange place. Depending on your cat's personality, she may become stressed if she's taken from familiar surroundings and could feel that she's been abandoned.

Making a Final Decision

Always take your cat's feelings into consideration when the need to travel arises.

Take Me With You!

Some owners still believe that it's better to rehome the family cat when they have to move a great distance or go away to school. This seems odd to me. If you are about to make this decision, I ask you to reconsider. Here are some things to think about:

- If you moved, you wouldn't give away your kids, would you? Your cat considers you to be her pack, so it would be very traumatizing for her to be taken away from her family.
- Cats really aren't a hassle when moving. You can easily transport them by car or even by airplane in a carrier.
- Believe it or not, your cat will adjust to a new home in time. Your company and attention, along with the scent of familiar things, will help ease her through the transition. Bring some of her old toys along, and try rubbing her blanket on different items to disperse her scent throughout her new surroundings. Using pheromones will also make things go a bit easier.

Owners now have the option to board their pets at luxury pet hotels and inns. These deluxe accommodations offer spacious suites, toys, special spa services, and personal attention.

Most cats won't enjoy a vacation. Besides, you'll have a better trip knowing that your cat is happier being well taken care of in her comfy, familiar surroundings while you're gone. And you'll probably come home to a more content and grateful cat.

SO NOW YOU KNOW...

- Many cats detest traveling because they're basically homebodies by nature.
- You can get your cat used to traveling by taking her on short, fun trips. It's easier to train her to accept travel when she is a kitten.
- To prevent unnecessary hassles, you must contact the airlines regarding rules and regulations when flying with a pet.
- For her overall safety, your cat should be microchipped and registered with a known microchip registry, especially if you expect to travel often with her.
- To ensure your cat's well-being when she must be away from home, always pack a kitty travel kit that includes all the daily essential items she uses, including her litter box, litter, and food.
- If your cat truly detests traveling, it may be best to leave her at home with a pet sitter or to board her at a "cat-only" kennel.

Appendix A: Cat Breed Personality Profiles

These are general descriptions of cat breed personalities, but there are always variations within the breeds, depending on the individual cat. For example, a normally active and playful Abyssinian could be shy or laid back, or the quiet and docile Persian could be a rowdy character. Age, health, and genetics will affect activity levels and other personality traits.

Abyssinian

Abyssinians are busy and active cats. Always playful and always in the middle of things, they are born athletes and get into things all the time. They love toys but can and often do make anything a toy. They are fearless by nature, and—not always in their best interest—they like heights. Because these cats are so energetic, a lone Abyssinian is asking for trouble. She needs constant companionship, like another cat or even a dog who has been properly introduced to be her playmate.

American Bobtail

American Bobtails are smart and adaptable. Some have been known to open doors or sneak off with shiny objects, so you may have a challenge when dealing with these cats. They love to play fetch, hide-and-seek, and myriad other games—some of which they'll make up. These cats, whether young or old, tend to be interested in spending time with their humans, and they can get along well with most other pets.

American Curl

The American Curl has a sweet and adaptable personality. Playful and always wanting to be in the middle of things, this breed bonds easily with humans and usually gets along well with other pets, given the right introductions. Their behavior remains kitten-like throughout their adult life.

American Shorthair

The American Shorthair is friendly and affectionate, but unlike some cats who may be clingy, these felines can entertain themselves for a time. They're generally good with other pets, given the right introductions, and they enjoy human companionship. Calm and loving, their personality belies their fierceness in mousing, which they will do whenever given the opportunity.

American Wirehair

The American Wirehair is known for being quiet and reserved yet playful and inquisitive at the same time. They're very affectionate and look for attention wherever they can find it. They can be clever, too, able to open up cabinets and climb inside, so childproof latches are a must with this intelligent and curious breed. They will generally get along with other pets, given the right introductions.

Balinese

Balinese are social cats with a lot of voice. They will often try to carry on a conversation with you and will demand attention if they think that you're ignoring them. Balinese are extremely intelligent, curious, and loving. In fact, their behavior and loyalty often resemble that of a dog in that they follow their owners everywhere they go, staying by their side or on their laps, wanting to be in the middle of whatever they're doing. Agile, swift, and active, they also love to play games.

They get along easily with other pets and yet are independent enough to handle being alone.

Birman

Birman cats are not quite as active as many of the other Oriental breeds, but they are not as laid back as some of the larger longhaired cats. They are charming, gentle, and playful but quiet and unobtrusive if you are busy with other things. Generally easygoing and relaxed, they remain playful into old age and at times may demand your attention; however, they will happily settle down nearby once they get it. Very social creatures, their life revolves around the family that they love. These sweet-natured cats make great pets for children. Another pet, whether a cat or dog, is usually welcomed.

Bombay

Bombay cats are middle of the road when it comes to activity level. They're smart, curious, and always happy to play but aren't as rambunctious as some breeds. They like to play fetch and will investigate anything and everything that is fair game. Bombays love attention and often like to be carried about or to ride on your shoulder. They will often follow you from room to room and will almost always have something to say about what you are doing. Very attached to their owners, Bombays tend to love the entire family rather than bond with only one person, and they are particularly good with children. They can get along with other pets with the right introductions.

British Shorthair

The British Shorthair is laid back and always in quiet control of her environment, supervising everyone and everything that happens in the family. They are a bit reserved and dignified, so if you're looking for a quiet, steadfast companion who is affectionate and not hyperactive, this breed may be for you. They are easygoing and intelligent but won't be very demanding of your attention, although they will seek out play if they think that you're interested. These cats tend to get along with other cats and dogs.

Burmese

The Burmese is extremely charming and people-oriented. Their personalities are almost dog-like given their tendency to follow their owners around, wanting to both bestow and receive affection. Burmese will enjoy being with you to cuddle and socialize all day. They also take great pleasure in helping to "manage" the household, either taking an active role or preferring to supervise from the lap position. They can be stubborn and difficult if they want to do something you don't want them to do. If emotionally slighted by their owner, they may sulk a bit but will get over it quickly. They are good with children, and they will get along with other cats and dogs if they're introduced early enough in their lives.

Chartreux

Known for its smile and bright eyes, the Chartreux is a reserved and quiet cat who seldom meows but who will speak in the form of other noises similar to a chirp when it finds something interesting. Most do not like to be picked up or carried. As kittens and adolescents, they are active but calm down after about three years of age. Even as adults, they will have bursts of activity, although they are largely known for their regal behavior. Chartreux quickly become attached to their family and frequently follow loved ones from room to room; they can be shy around new people, though. These cats can do well with other pets if introduced properly.

Colorpoint Shorthair

The Colorpoint Shorthair is a highly interactive and talkative breed. Very active and always into exploring things, these cats are quite smart and trainable. If you're looking for a cat to do tricks or try agility, a Colorpoint would probably be a good choice. These are playful, fun-loving cats who thrive on company and require a fair amount of attention from you. If you aren't home during the day, it's best to keep them with cats of their own activity level or in busy households where they are left alone for long periods.

They can get along with most pets given the right introductions.

Cornish Rex

Cornish Rex are smart yet clownish, entertaining their owners with their antics for quite a while. They can be exceedingly vocal, so it's very important not to respond to their vocalizations if you wish to have a quieter cat. Active busybodies who are also excellent jumpers and climbers, they are counter creepers and food raiders, so you must vigilantly enforce boundaries with them. They also like to steal objects and retrieve them. Not quiet lap cats, they prefer to live in a home in which they can exercise their relentless energy. Even though they are extremely independent, they love to be petted and handled and they are even known to be excessively fond of dogs!

Devon Rex

The Devon Rex is highly active and playful, wanting to be involved in whatever is going on in your household and often inviting themselves to be part of every activity. Little escapes their interest, and very few spots will go unexplored or unoccupied. They are often found climbing bookcases and perching on top of doors.

Powerful jumpers, they are also known to be counter creepers and food moochers, so expect to enforce boundaries, especially when it comes to your meal. Extremely friendly, Devons never met anyone they didn't like. They love snuggling and cuddling, preferring to be perched on a shoulder, lap, or wherever they can be closest to their people, so you'll need to show extra affection with this feline. They do well with other pets given the proper introductions.

Egyptian Mau

The Egyptian Mau is a shy and reserved cat, but once you enter her heart, she is forever yours. An extremely delightful and intelligent animal, Maus place great importance on family and are fiercely loyal in their devotion to them. They can be quite active or very quiet, depending on their mood. They are great leapers, so expect a fair amount of jumping and climbing. The Mau is normally very good with other pets.

European Burmese

An elegant but not fragile cat, the European Burmese has a sweet disposition. Highly intelligent, affectionate, and extremely loyal, these cats make outstanding pets. They crave companionship and will love being with you to cuddle and socialize all day. European Burmese also enjoy the company of another animal; however, they can live quite happily as the sole pet. They tend to be middle of the road in terms of their activity level, although they remain playful and energetic throughout adulthood. They can do clever things like play fetch and enjoy supervising you when you are doing household chores.

Exotic

The Exotic is the shorthaired version of the Persian and has the same temperament as one.

They are quiet, affectionate, and docile. They can be reserved, especially with strangers. Unlike many cats, they respect your "space" and will not demand attention constantly. They will follow you from room to room but aren't pushy. Easygoing and peaceful by nature, they are nevertheless just as playful and fun-loving as other breeds. They may entertain themselves until exhausted trying to catch a toy on a stick, or they'll happily sit calmly studying it for next time. They can get along with other pets given the right introductions.

Havana Brown

Moderately active, the Havana Brown has a charming, playful demeanor and a soft voice. Many Havanas can be aloof and shy, so socialization is a must when they are kittens. The more outgoing ones can be a bit chatty, however, so be aware of this aspect of their nature if you want a quiet pet. Havanas often like to use their paws to investigate things they are curious about by touching and feeling them. A people-oriented breed, they quietly demand human companionship and adapt well to most situations. This is the perfect cat for the person who wants a sociable, affectionate, and intelligent feline friend. They can get along with other pets with the right introductions.

Japanese Bobtail

If you're looking for an active, intelligent, and talkative cat, look no farther than the Japanese Bobtail. These cats adore human companionship, and their soft voices are capable of nearly a whole scale of tones. Some people say they sing and almost always speak when spoken to. They are extremely active and playful, getting into anything and everything and seemingly always looking for trouble. Because they're so smart,

they are adept at opening cabinets and doors and getting into things they shouldn't—so cabinet latches are a must. Master pouncers, their high energy level and dexterity make them good mousers and agility cats. They are especially good with children and can get along with other pets with the right introductions.

Javanese

This is a breed for people who want a little spice in their life. Javanese are social cats with a lot of voice. They will even try to carry on a conversation with you and loudly demand attention if they think you're ignoring them. They are highly intelligent and quickly become familiar with your routine. They will often speak their minds to let you know what they need, whether it's a meal or just some attention. Although Javanese appear fragile, they are actually quite muscular and capable of acrobatic feats. Considered a "busy" breed, they often seem to have nothing better to do than follow you around and get underfoot—yet they will delight in entertaining you with silly antics. Most seem to like dogs, if introduced properly, as well as other pets.

Korat

The Korat is highly intelligent and expressive. Having extraordinary powers of hearing, sight, and scent, they're keen observers who are capable of opening doors and cabinets, turning on water faucets, and opening containers with lids. They can become quite active at times, and they love to play fetch and other games. However, they are gentle, sensitive pets who tend to move quietly and cautiously, and so they dislike unexpected loud or harsh noises. Extremely affectionate, Korats form exceptionally strong bonds with their owners and respond warmly to cuddling. They get along well with other cats but tend to want to have the upper hand and won't let anyone keep them from their rightful place at their owner's side. They are very gentle with children.

LaPerm

The LaPerm are affectionate cats who love to touch and be touched. They can be extremely active but also love being lap cats, so the two traits are not mutually exclusive in this breed. These cats will often follow your lead in terms of seeking interaction; if you're busy, they will wait patiently for you to give them some attention or playtime—although they will sometimes seek out contact by rubbing up against you or patting you with their paws. Inquisitive by nature, they always want to know what's going on around them. They can get along with other pets with the right introductions.

Maine Coon Cat

The Maine Coon Cat is the gentle giant of cats. Very sociable, strong, and tranquil, some are bigger in size than many small dogs. They're often compared with dogs in temperament as well. Known for their kindly disposition, these cats are never too pushy, and they make affectionate and easygoing companions. They are especially good with children and dogs.

Manx

The Manx is outgoing and friendly. Particularly playful, these cats love playing with their humans, often bringing them toys and looking for a game of fetch. They are also very athletic and can jump amazingly high. It's not unusual to find them perched at the highest point in the room. Sometimes referred to as "feline sports cars," they are able to accelerate and make quick turns. Affectionate and loving, Manx cats are devoted to their families but reserved around strangers. However, once they bond with their owners, it is difficult for many Manx to be happy in a different home. They can get along with other pets with the right introductions.

Norwegian Forest Cat

The Norwegian Forest Cat is friendly, lively, and full of personality. Intelligent and incurably curious, they can be quite active during playtime. They love to investigate everything and never want to miss out on things, so they may not easily accept that certain places are off-limits to them. You may find this habit challenging at times and should set some strict boundaries. While many Wegies are not lap cats, they are still highly affectionate, enjoying petting and human contact. They love to stick close by you, but when the weather is hot, they prefer instead to curl up at your side because of their thick coats. They thrive in the company of other cats and will usually share their home with a dog. Even-tempered and not generally nervous or easily startled, they make good pets for children.

Ocicat

Ocicats are not part ocelot, as some people may infer from the name, but rather a wild-looking cat with tame genes. There is no wild or feral cat in them. They are devoted and affectionate cats but not too clingy or demanding. Very confident and bright, Ocicats are capable of being trained and will respond well to commands. Some may even learn to walk on a leash. Because they are adaptable, they will usually comply willingly once they understand the house rules. They tend to be extroverts, but their sociable nature may make them less likely to do well if left alone for long periods. They enjoy being with other animals, provided, of course, that they are properly introduced.

Oriental

Orientals have rather vibrant personalities. Intensely curious and a bit too nosy, these cats always seem to be there to nudge you or interrupt your activities. Affectionate and loving, they will try to claim you as their own and are not too interested in sharing you, but they will repay you by providing company and a comforting purr or nuzzle when you need it. They'll do anything to please you and crave your attention—and if they don't get it, they will limp about sadly, making a display of their disappointment. Orientals tend to be extremely vocal when they don't get what they want. Despite their extremely social nature, they will get along well enough when you're not around. When bored, though, they will stick their pusses into drawers and closets looking for something with which to distract themselves. This means that you'll need to secure areas in which you don't want them to snoop. Oriental cats will remain playful and spirited long into old age.

Persian

Persians are quiet, affectionate, and docile. They can be aloof, especially with strangers. Unlike many cats, they respect your "space" and will not demand constant attention. They will follow you from room to room but aren't pushy. Creatures of habit, they feel most comfortable and secure in a tranquil environment but can adapt to most noisy, active households with lots of attention and reassurance. Although mellow and reserved, don't be surprised to find your Persian posing rather elegantly in your favorite chair or draped dramatically on the windowsill for all to see. These responsive and pleasant cats make good companions, and they can get along well with other pets.

Ragamuffin

Like the Maine Coon, Ragamuffins are gentle giants. They are very sociable, strong, and tranquil—some are bigger than many small dogs. They're in some ways compared to dogs, often playing a game of fetch. Not too pushy, they are affectionate and easygoing. They will often go limp in your arms if you pick one up, hence the name. They can get along with other pets with the right introductions.

Ragdoll

Like the Maine Coon and Ragamuffin, Ragdolls are massive cats who display a calm, gentle manner. They are very sociable, strong, and tranquil and tend to be more interested in humans than many other breeds are. They're often compared to dogs because they will run to greet you, follow you around, sleep with you, and often invite you to play a game of your choice. They tend to be floor cats and are not inclined to jumping or climbing. Never pushy, these cats are affectionate, easygoing, and well-behaved companions. They're exceedingly sweet and laid back—great for a person who wants a quieter cat. They can get along with other pets with the right introductions.

Russian Blue

Russian Blues are shy, unassuming, and quiet cats. Once they become part of your life, though, you will find them affectionate and loyal. They are generally not high-activity cats; they will entertain themselves if left alone for the day and be a contented companion upon your return. Many enjoy being lap and shoulder kitties. Very sensitive creatures, they perceive what is going on around them and will try to cheer you up by clowning around or will stay out of your way if you don't want company. However, they're smart and a bit stubborn, so if they decide that they want to do something, you may have a bit of a battle on your hands. They can get along with children and other pets with the right introductions.

Scottish Fold

The Scottish Fold is a moderately active cat who is neither aloof nor clingy. Hardy and playful, these cats need lots of affection as well as play. They adore spending time with their humans and will settle for quietly keeping you company if you are not in the mood to entertain them. They have tiny voices and tend not to be very vocal, so you can enjoy a quiet evening together. Most Scottish Folds do well with other pets, but introductions to other cats must be made carefully. Many cats look on the Scottish Fold's folded ears as a sign of aggression, so introductions must be slow and deliberate. Nevertheless, they will adjust to other animals and adapt well to most home environments.

Selkirk Rex

The Selkirk Rex is a fun-loving and clownish cat who enjoys playing above all else. She loves attention, especially when you play with her. Selkirk Rexes are active cats, so keep this in mind if you choose to get one. However, they love to cuddle, so be aware that they need their quiet time, too. They can get along with other pets with the right introductions.

Siamese

In the cat dictionary under the word "vocal," you will see a picture of the Siamese. Yes, they are *that* vocal. You can reduce some of the chattiness by not reacting to it, but that may be a lost cause. Siamese are inquisitive and busy cats. Always into exploring and extremely intelligent, they'll never pass up the chance to let you know what they're thinking. Rather affectionate by nature, they will also require a fair amount of attention from you and will enjoy being your constant companion. Siamese can get along with other pets with the right introductions.

Siberian

Siberians are generally mellow, affectionate cats. They enjoy being lap cats and are usually quiet, with the occasional soft vocalization. They will follow you everywhere, so you'll never be alone with this feline companion. Siberians can be active while playing but are happy to sit with you and watch television. However, they are quite agile and can leap great distances and heights, and because they are great problem solvers, you can expect the unexpected living with this super sleuth. Siberians are usually good with dogs and other cats with the proper introductions.

Singapura

Singapuras are endearing and pleasantly pesky cats. Curious and extremely playful, these extroverts want to be at the center of everything, whether you're cooking, working on the computer, or reading a book. They are intelligent and interactive with people well into old age, and despite their nosy tendencies, tend to be non-destructive, making them fun to have as housemates. They can get along with other pets with the right introductions.

Somali

Somalis thrive on human attention and are extremely social. Born athletes, they love to play and are likely to have bursts of energy throughout the day, during which they will scamper about tossing toys and jumping into the air like acrobats. They can even hold objects with their paws and are adept at getting into cabinets and raiding food from counters, so you may have your work cut out for you if you own one. They are often fearless—and not always in their best interest—and like heights. Because these cats are so active, keeping a lone Somali is asking for trouble. These cats need constant companionship—another cat or even a dog who has been properly introduced would be a good playmate while you are away from home.

Sphynx

Sphynx cats are loving cats who demand human attention—in fact, they may even perform tricks and silly antics to get it. They often become extremely attached to their humans. Almost flirtatious, they love strangers, too, and will often greet and even hop on them to say hello. Smart, clever, and mischievous, most enjoy interactive games but tend to be a bit clumsy at times. Sphynxes are excellent counter creepers who are capable of getting into cabinets and climbing on counters, so you may have your work cut out for you if you own one. They love the company of other cats and dogs.

Tonkinese

Tonkinese are affectionate but strong-willed cats with a penchant for getting into mischief. They love testing boundaries, so training for counter creeping and other behaviors is highly recommended. Even so, they are playful and athletic and want to be at the center of everything—and they can quickly take over both your house and your life if you let them. They are also very intelligent and have senses similar to radar, so don't be surprised if your Tonk is always playing hide-and-seek with you. Constantly seeking entertainment, these cats tend to be charmers and do well with strangers and other pets.

Turkish Angora

Turkish Angoras are lively and loving cats. Most are a bit headstrong, so training and socialization are vitally important. They're intelligent and love to play but can be a bit intense for the owner who is looking for a cat who is more docile. They can open doors, cabinets, and drawers and have a great affinity for clearing a table of knickknacks. Interestingly, many of these cats like water and will try to bathe with their owners. They are usually good with dogs and other cats but tend to be assertive and will try to be in charge, so proper introductions are crucial.

Turkish Van

Turkish Vans are loyal, loving, but very independent cats. They are known to display affection by butting you with their heads and giving you little love bites, which may be disconcerting until you get to know them as such. They're intelligent and love to play but can be a bit clumsy, wreaking havoc on fragile vases and glassware or knocking over houseplants. Agile and quite strong, these cats are great climbers and can open cabinets and drawers; they also wouldn't think twice about climbing your curtains. Many Turkish Vans swim or at least like water, so don't be surprised to find them in the swimming pool or investigating the toilet a bit too closely. These cats are not lap cats and will need firm boundaries. They can be bullies with other cats and other dogs without proper socialization and training.

Appendix B:
Pet Products, Services, and Training Resources

Affordable Cat Fence
722 West Kings Highway
San Antonio, Texas, 78212
(888) 840-2287
www.catfence.com

Alley Cat Allies
7920 Norfolk Avenue
Suite 600
Bethesda, MD 20814-2525
(240) 482-1980
www.alleycat.org

Cat Enclosure Kit
C & D Pet Products LLC
405 East D Street
Petaluma, CA 94952
(707) 763-1654
(888) 554-7387
www.cdpets.com

Cat Fence-In
P.O. Box 795 Dept. E
Sparks, NV 89432
(888) 738-9099
www.catfencein.com

CozyCatFurniture.com
Peshoni LLC
220 E. Delaware Avenue
Newark, DE 19711
(302) 309-9183
info@cozycatfurniture.com
www.cozycatfurniture.com

Feline Furniture Company
P.O. Box 3379
Lake Arrowhead, CA 92352
909-336-9414
909-336-9410 (fax)
felinefurniture@gmail.com
www.felinefurniture.com

Friends of Animals
(800) 321-PETS
www.friendsofanimals.org

Home Again Recovery System
P.O. Box 2014
East Syracuse, NY 13057-4514
(866) 738-4324
www.homeagain.com

House of Cats International
25011 Bell Mountain Drive
San Antonio, TX 78255
(800) 889-7402
(210) 698-3329 (fax)
www.houseofcatsintl.com

**International Association of
Animal Behavior Consultants (IAABC)**
505 Timber Lane
Jefferson Hills, PA 15025
www.iaabc.org

KatWALLks
Off the Wall Cat Furniture by Burdworks
P.O. Box 239

Wynona, OK 74084
(877) 644-1615
katwallks@earthlink.com
www.katwallks.com

Kittywalk
Pet Rageous Products Inc.
20 Blanchard Road Suite 11
Burlington, MA 01803
(866) 829-0504
www.kittywalk.com

Littermaid Litterbox
www.littermaid.com

National Dog Registry (for all pets)
P.O. Box 116
Woodstock, NY 12498
(800) 637-3647
www.natldogregistry.com

Omega Paw Self-Cleaning Litterbox
Radio Fence Distributors, Inc.
1133 Bal Harbor Blvd, Suite 1153
Punta Gorda, FL 33950
(800) 941-4200
www.radiofence.com

Petfinder.com
www.petfinder.com

Playtime Workshop
406 Hawk St. STE D
Rockledge, FL 32955
Phone: 321-631-9246
customerservice@playtimeworkshop.com
www.playtimeworkshop.com

Purrfect Cat Fence
Benner's Purr-fect Fence
201 Fayette Street
Conshohocken, PA 19428
888.280.4066
www.purrfectfence.com

Purrforma Plus Litterbox
Petmate
P.O. Box 1246
Arlington, Texas USA 76004-1246
(877) 738-6283
www.petmate.com

SPAY USA
(800) 248-SPAY
www.spayusa.org

Spoil My Kitty, LLC.
4278 New Irvine Rd.
Waco, KY 40385
(888) 403-2859
www.spoilmykitty.com

Tattoo-a-Pet
6571 S.W. 20th Court
Ft. Lauderdale, FL 33317
(800) 828-8667
www.tattoo-a-pet.com

The Litter Robot
Automated Pet Care Products, Inc.
40 W Howard St, Suite B-5
Pontiac, Michigan 48342
(877) 250-7729
www.litter-robot.com

Resources

Registry Organizations

American Association of Cat Enthusiasts (AACE)
P.O. Box 213
Pine Brook, NJ 07058
Phone: (973) 335-6717
Website: www.aaceinc.org

American Cat Fanciers Association (ACFA)
P.O. Box 1949
Nixa, MO 65714
Phone: (417) 725-1530
Website: www.acfacat.com

Canadian Cat Association (CCA)
289 Rutherford Road South
Unit 18
Brampton, Ontario, Canada
L6W 3R9
Phone: (905) 459-1481
Website: www.cca-afc.com

The Cat Fanciers' Association (CFA)
1805 Atlantic Avenue
P.O. Box 1005
Manasquan, NJ 08736-0805
Phone: (732) 528-9797
Website: www.cfainc.org

The Governing Council of the Cat Fancy (GCCF)
4-6, Penel Orlieu
Bridgwater, Somerset, TA6 3PG
UK
Phone: +44 (0)1278 427 575
Website: ourworld.compuserve.com/homepages/GCCF_CATS/

The International Cat Association (TICA)
P.O. Box 2684
Harlingen, TX 78551
Phone: (956) 428-8046
Website: www.tica.org

Veterinary Specialty/ Membership Organizations

Academy of Veterinary Homeopathy (AVH)
P.O. Box 9280
Wilmington, DE 19809
Phone: (866) 652-1590
Website: www.theavh.org

American Holistic Veterinary Medical Association (AHVMA)
2214 Old Emmorton Road
Bel Air, MD 21015
Phone: (410) 569-0795
Website: www.ahvma.org

American Veterinary Medical Association (AVMA)
1931 North Meacham Road, Suite 100
Schaumburg, IL 60173
Phone: (847) 925-8070
Website: www.avma.org

The American Association for Veterinary Acupuncture (AAVA)
P.O. Box 419
Hygiene, CO 80533
Phone: (303) 772-6726
Website: www.aava.org

Animal Behavior Associates, Inc.
4994 South Independence Way
Littleton, CO 80123
Phone: (303) 932-9095
Website: www. animalbeahvior-associates.com

ASPCA Animal Poison Control Center
1717 South Philo Road, Suite 36
Urbana, IL 61802
Telephone: (888) 426-4435
Website: www.aspca.org

Cornell Feline Health Center
College of Veterinary Medicine
Cornell University, Box 13
Ithaca, NY 14853
Phone: (607) 253-3414
Website: web.vet.cornell.edu/public/fhc/FelineHealth.html

International Association of Animal Behavior Consultants (IAABC)
505 Timber Lane
Jefferson Hills, PA 15025
Website: www.iaabc.org

Animal Welfare Groups and Organizations

Alley Cat Allies
1801 Belmont Road NW, Suite 201
Washington, DC 20009
Phone: (202) 667-3630
Website: www.alleycat.org

American Humane Association (AHA)
63 Inverness Drive East
Englewood, CO 80112
Phone: (800) 227-4645
Website: www.americanhu-mane.org

American Society for the Prevention of Cruelty to Animals (ASPCA)
424 East 92 Street
New York, NY 10128
Phone: (212) 876-7700
Website: www.aspca.org

Cats Protection
17 Kings Road
Horsham, West Sussex RH13 5PN UK
Phone: +44 (0) 1403 221900
Website: www.cats.org.uk

Feral Cat Coalition
9528 Miramar Road, PMB 160
San Diego, CA 92126
Phone: (619) 497-1599
Website: www.feralcat.com

The Humane Society of the United States (HSUS)
2100 L Street, NW
Washington, DC 20037
Phone: (212) 452-1100
Website: www.hsus.org

Websites

American Veterinary Society of Animal Behavior
www.avsabonline.com

This organization is made up of a group of veterinarians and research professionals who share an interest in understanding behavior in animals.

Animal Behavior Associates
www.animalbehaviorassociates.com

Certified and degreed applied animal behaviorists provide behavior counseling using the power of the latest scientific information to help you understand and change your pet's behavior

Publications

Books
Bonham, Maggie. *Bring Me Home: Cats Make Great Pets*, Howell Book House, 2005.

Bonham, Maggie. *Bring Me Home: Dogs Make Great Pets*, Howell Book House, 2005.

Bonham, Maggie. *The Simple Guide to Getting Active With Your Dog*, TFH Publications, 2002.

Fields-Babineau, Miriam. *Cat Training in 10 Minutes*, TFH Publications, Inc, 2003.

Morgan, Diane, *Good Catkeeping*, TFH Publications, Inc, 2007.

Pryor, Karen. *Getting Started: Clicker Training for Cats*, Sunshine Books, 2001.

Webster-Boneham, Sheila. *Senior Cats*, TFH Publications, Inc, 2007.

Wilkins, Kelli A. *Cats*, TFH Publications, Inc,

Index

Note: **Boldfaced** numbers indicate illustrations.

About the Author

Margaret H. Bonham, world-renowned pet expert and author, has published 20 books and has written numerous articles for pet magazines. She has also won the Maxwell Award three times for writing excellence, the Muse Medallion from the Cat Writers' Association for best health and care book, and the IAMS Responsible Cat Ownership Award for her book *Bring Me Home: Cats Make Great Pets*. Maggie is a member of the National Writers Association and the Cat Writers' Association. She lives in Conifer, Colorado with her dogs and cat.

Photo Credits